Today "i" MUST Confess

"THE GOSPEL
ACCORDING TO RELIGION & POLITICS."
BY YOURS TRULY, DR. SUNDAY

A different kind of church
discover where you fit in

((ANSWERS TO MYSTERIOUS END OF AN AGE PROPHECY FULFILLED))

DR. SUNDAY

AuthorHouse™
1663 Liberty Drive
Bloomington, IN 47403
www.authorhouse.com
Phone: 1-800-839-8640

First published by AuthorHouse   11/17/2011

ISBN: 978-1-4490-0306-7 (sc)

Library of Congress Control Number: 2011960593

Printed in the United States of America

Any people depicted in stock imagery provided by Thinkstock are models, and such images are being used for illustrative purposes only.
Certain stock imagery © Thinkstock.

This book is printed on acid-free paper.

Celebrate America

☞ DO YOU SUPPORT
FREEDOM OF CHOICE
or FREEDOM OF speech?

A Storypath To *Safeguard*

AMERICAN WRITERS INSTITUTE PROUDLY PRESENTS

journalist Release of

SPIRITUALLY MOTIVATED

A BOOK OF CHAPTERIZED ESSAYS

31 YEARS IN THE MAKING

STACK PAGES HAVE IT ALL

BIBLIOGRAPHY

MOMENTS IN HISTORY

ENLIGHTENING VIEWS

Answer to

highway to heaven DIRECTIONS ➡

"where to begin"
A PROMISE FULFILLED
DELIVERS
imagemakers
"Stop this cover-up!"

" HIS TIME IS NOW / END OF DAZE, METER IS RUNNING "

NORMALCY ANYONE? ARMAGEDDON TO YOU YET!?

"" YOU NEED ME. "" SIGNED: YOURS TRULY, THE ANTI-CHRIST.

"BOOK'S PARALLEL EPILOGUE: AND DEAR GOD, NO NEED TO

FORGIVE ANYONE NOW = FOR THEY NOW KNOW WHAT THEY DO!"...

Give'em some of that new-time religion
"Presenting GOD'S INSPIRED WORD."

((TO ALL MY RELIGIOUS COMPETITORS.))

""WHEN YOUR DOGMA QUITS BARKING""

FREEDOM OF CHOICE' IS FOR YOU TO PREACH 'MY GOSPEL AND KEEP ALL YOUR

$$$ PARISHIONERS, OR SUFFER THE CONSECQUNCES OF HEAVY DUTY COMPETITION.

MANUSCRIPT CLONING SCHOOL IS Not The Same Old Song And Dance

Don't Touch That Dial
"STOP THE WORLD I, WANT TO GET ON."

LIVING IN A WORLD WHERE ((THERE'S ONLY 'ONE)) PEACEFUL
REVOLUTIONARY ((TICKET INTO THIS)) CHANGE THE WORLD FOR
THE BETTERMENT OF MANKIND ((ARENA.)) WHEREAS FOR ALL THE
REST OF MY CHALLENGING ADVERSATIVE, NON- PACKAGE DEALING,
— 'JESUS PROCLAIMERS; —

THERE EITHER IN THE NUT HOUSE, OR THEY BELONG THERE!

SIGNED: YOURS TRULY, (666.) "NOBODY EVER WANTED TO BE ME".

FACT IS I'M ABOUT AS THREATENING AS A DEVILED EGG. A WAKE-
UP CALL EXHIBIT.(INSX-MANIFEST-SONG) 'EVERYONE THE DEVIL

A Storypath To CHALLENGE!   INSIDE!!!

DEVIL'S FOOD CAKE ANYONE??? THEREFORE IN RETROSPECT,

`THIS IS ONE BIG GOTCHA!!!

HISTORICALLY SPEAKING, WHEN YOU GET IT RIGHT THE FIRST TIME

WITH OVER 30, YEARS OF PROFOUND SPECTRAL AMMO

THEY'LL BE NO NEED FOR `MY 2ND COMING!!!

Thanks for the memories. ⟶

NATION-WIDE *Letters to the Editor* ETC.

((((FRIAR-FLYER-2011 'WARNING-BULLETIN.))))

THE SEARCH FOR SIGNS OF INTELLIGENT LIFE IN THE UNIVERSE??
STEP RIGHT UP ! GOD-WORKING-THRU-MAN-HERE-WITHIN-YOUR-PRAYERS-BEING-ANSWERED..
·FAMILY VALUES RUNAMUCK!!! RECOGNIZING UN-SUSTAINABLE 'GLOBAL POPULATION
GROWTH ANYONE? "WHAT WE HAVE 'HERE IS A FAILURE TO COMMUNICATE! 15 YEARS AGO,
I ALERTED THE MEDIA IN REFERENCE TO: PRO-LIFE, GOES INTO EFFECT THE DAY PRO-
INTELLIGENCE ((BIRTH CONTROL)) COMES OF AGE. IRRESPONSIBILITY CULMINATES TO
THIS HERE BEING A GLOBAL RESOURCE EXHAUSTING 'BABY FACTORY' POVERTY STRICKEN
OVER-LOAD OF =BIBLICAL PROPORTIONS=! -FETUS-FEED-US-FEET-US-(SHOES,etc.-FEAT-
·US-(JOBS, JOBS, JOBS,) COME'ON IN THE WATERS FINE, FOR GOODNESS SNAKE...

"IN RETROSPECT,
'INFLATION' IS QUALITY OF LIFE'S WORST NIGHTMARE"
((P R I C E - G O U G I N G - D O M I N O - E F F E C T))
HOW SOON WE FORGET THAT EGYPT'S UPRISE STARTED WITH INFLATION
OVER-ALL MID-EAST ♩ WHEN YOU GOT NOTHING,YOU GOT NOTHING TO LOSE.
UPHEAVAL.
¢¢¢ IRRELIGIOUS LEADERSHIP ANYONE? "FOR THE TRUE LOVE OF GOD"
LET THERE BE STRENGTH IN NUMBERS! PEACEFUL EVOLUTION, REVOLUTION
IS THE SOLUTION, TO BE FREE OF MENTAL POLUTION; - ANSWERS TO -
DEMOCRACY
ANYONE ??? "REPENT AND SPREAD THE SUSTAINABLE "WEALTH AMEN.¢¢¢
= THINKING OUT SIDE THE BOX, BOOK FORETELLING OF MIRACLES =
(DOMESTICALLY SPEAKING)
"CAN YOU SAY 'YOU HAVE A LEGITIMATE PLAN THAT CAN
SOLVE ALL OF THE UN- EMPLOYMENT PROBLEMS IN THIS
COUNTRY? NO! 'I CAN... CAN YOU SAY THAT 'YOU
HAVE A LEGITIMATE PLAN THAT WILL BALANCE THE FEDERAL
BUDGET DEFICIT,'AND THEN SOME? NO! 'I CAN.
CAN YOU SAY 'YOU HAVE A LEGITIMATE HEALTH CARE
PROPOSAL WITHOUT ROCKING THE STATUS QUO BOAT. NO!'I CAN!
ON- OBAMA CARE! AS IT STANDS "REPEL THIS EDSEL"
-STATEMENT-COMPLETE-PROPOSALS-REVISITED-IN-BOOK-!!!-
FURTHERMORE IN BRIEF: POSITIVE EARTH. = NEGATIVE EARTH. 9.0 EARTHQUAKE
IS LIKE THAT OF BEING AN ACT OF A GROUND GAINING NEGATIVE godZILLA;
TOSS IN THE FALSE god WORSHIPING OF CHRISTCHURCH, FOR A KICKER!!!
AUTHOR DISCOVERY??? EXPERIENCE THE DIFFERENCE OF YOURS TRULY
ANTI-JESUS, AND THE 'JUSTIFIABLE "ALL GOD'S CHILDREN" EXPRESS,
FOUNDER OF THE POSITIVE FAITH RELIGION; HEAVEN ON EARTH EDUCATOR.
MEDIA FRENZY, FLY ON THE WALL TAPED INTERVIEWS ANYONE???
'THY WILL BE DONE " APPOINTMENT REMINDER'
OUTTA THIS WORLD AND ON WITH THE NEXT??
ANSWERS TO MYSTERIOUS END OF AN AGE PROPHECY FULFILLED
A MEDIA POSTED, OR PUBLICIZED GATHERING EVENT???
TIME AND PLACE IS YOUR CALL!!
WELCOME TO RENO NEVADA ...

LETTUCE  PREY

BASED ON THE PROLIFERATE TEACHINGS OF A MORALIST! -(2009)-

"PRESIDENT OBAMA, ((WHO DOSEN'T ANSWER HIS MAIL.)) SEEMS TO THINK
THAT BUSINESS AS USUAL 'EDUCATION IS THE ANSWER" DAAAAAA--- AND
ALL THOSE GOLDEN PARACHUTE BAILOUT SHARPIES, ALONG WITH EVERYONE
FROM MADOFF TO MARKOFF ETC, WERE HIGHLY EDUCATED PEOPLE!---
PROVING THAT "FIRST AND FOREMOST THE PRIORITY OF A+ EDUCATION
IS THAT OF BEING A MORAL ONE." THEREFORE ENTER 'ASPIRING T,V,
MINISTRIES FINENESS IN PROGRAMING AND ENTERTAINMENT.
THE DR. SUNDAY SHOW!

ALL God's Children

"INDIVIDUAL RESPONSIBILITY" TOWARDS THE BETTERMENT OF MANKIND...
CHALLENGING ALL THOSE
NEANDERTHAL RELIGIONS
(VERSUS)
YOURS TRULYS,
AN EXACT-A-MUNDO RELIGION...
"THE GOSPEL ACCORDING TO YOURS TRULY:

ALWAYS WAS AND ALWAYS WILL BE GOO IS
THE UNIVERSE LENDER, OMNIPOTENT SPENDER
AND MENDER OF HEARTS THAT ARE TENDER,
PURE LOVE'S ONE AND ONLY SENDER,
"THE POSITIVE SPIRIT WITHOUT GENDER".
FOUDROYANTLY, SO MANY WOMEN TO
RELIGIOUSLY EMANCIPATE,-SO LITTLE TIME.
PROPITIOUSLY AN EQUAL OPPORTUNITY EMPLOYER".

THEREFORE STICK IT WHERE THE 'SON, DON'T SHINE?! GLOBALLY SPEAKING,
HISTORICALLY SPEAKING; "ONLY THRU ME" BY WAY OF 'MY RELIGION,
WILL WOMEN EVER HAVE THE OPPORTUNITY TO GAIN MAJOR STRIDES
TOWARDS EQUALITY...

WRITTEN BY : FOUNDER OF THE POSITIVE FAITH RELIGION (1980).
--- HEAVEN ON EARTH EDUCATOR, --- DOCTOR OF RELIGIOUS SCIENCE,

DR. SUNDAY...

TAX-PAYER EXTORTION!!!
THE REPUBLIC FOR WHICH IT STANDS.
(VERSUS)
DEMOCRACY FOR WHICH IT SHOULD STAND. ➞

What ever happened to 'for the good of the country'?
"All the News That's Fit to Print"

"DISCOVERY OF YOURS TRULY" "DISCOVERY OF YOURS TRULY"

Great news travels fast!
(YEAH, RIGHT)

WELCOME TO NEW-AGE POLITICAL AND RELIGIOUS

PLUTOCRATIC 'Exorcism'.

WHAT IS PRAYER ACCORDING TO THIS MAN'S RELIGION?

EVERYTHING IN LIFE IS TO A DEGREE; IF YOU ARE PATIENT, YOU CAN
MODIFY YOUR OWN BEHAVIOR. THE MAJORITY OF MY PRAYER IS IN MY
PERSONALITY AND DECISION MAKINGS, IT'S JUST ONE PLAY AFTER
ANOTHER --- BECAUSE TO A GOOD DEGREE I'VE ALWAYS KEPT THE
VILLAIN IN ME AS MY UNDERSTUDY... HOW RELIGIOUS AM I? BEING THE
MONK AMONG YA, I FIND MYSELF PRAYING TO GOD, FOR GUIDANCE ALL
THE TIME! --- IN-FACT THE ONLY TIME I EVER GET LONELY IS WHEN
I HAVE TO GO TO THE BATHROOM...

" CLINGING TO MY RELIGION WITHOUT ANY GUNS." 2008.

AUTHOR'S BIO: THE REASON I DON'T OWN A GUN, IS BECAUSE
THEY COST TO MUCH---I'D HAVE TO GO OUT AND BUY ME A
BRAND NEW TELEVISION EVERYWEEK...

HOW WERE MY GRADES IN SCHOOL?

EVERYTIME THEY GAVE ME A BLOOD TEST I GOT A+.

2009. FURTHERMORE SAVING THE TAX PAYERS BILLIONS, AND WORKING
AS AN INDPENDENT JOE THE PLUMBER, LOGICAL STIMULUS
PACKAGE ASSESSOR= THEY MISSED MY CALLING!
SIGNED: THEY CAN ONLY KILL ME ONCE.

LIVING IN THIS A PLUTOCRATIC SOCIETY, =PEOPLE UNITE=

WHEREAS "THE ONLY THING WE HAVE TO FEAR IS
THE LACK OF SIGNIFICANT FREE-SPEECH, OR DEMOCRACY."
THE SEARCH FOR SIGNS OF INTELLIGENT LIFE IN THE UNIVERSE?

---OR HELL,

WHAT'S A NICE GUY LIKE ME DOING IN A PLACE LIKE THIS???

A ""POSITIVE MIND"" IS A TERRIBLE THING TO WASTE /// WRITTEN BY,

OR NEWS MEDIA SIGNED, AND READY FOR THE ALL S-T-A-R-E GAME;

AS DR. SUNDAY, W-R-I-T-E-S OFF INTO THE SUNSET...

The Book That Reveals
The Whole Shocking Truth

VOTER ALERT !

on representation **Who Counts, & Who Don't** ?

WHERE WE ARE NOW

The Secret History **of** Plutocracy

(Government by the Rich.)

C H R O N I C L E S

HIGHLIGHT

The Second Coming
of Democracy

FACTORY TO YOU !

WE'VE COME A LONG WAY
SINCE CHARIOT RACING.

HAD ENOUGH
FEATURES

The Man Who Saved Democracy

The Untold Stories

The Muzzling OF the Press
A Voice Silenced !

Get ready for truth **support**

Inquiring Minds Want to Know: PAGE 3

READING REVOLUTION

"Storytelling on a grand scale"

Nobody beats him in blame game !

Based on Notebooks

Powerful Testimony

CHARTING A NEW COURSE

redefining our politics.

YOU ARE HERE

Objectivity

The Secret Societies

LAST DAYS OF

Downsizing Democracy

Featured Prize

THE HUMPTY DUMPTY

PLUTOCRATIC
SYSTEM

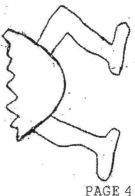

Vintage Journalism

The Wait Is Over.

MAXIMUM EXPOSURE *PREVENTION*

That was then...

The future of VOICE YOUR OPINIONS

IN AMERICA **speaking** out On Controversial Issues ?

"Great lessons in protests" PAGE 5

IN REPRESENTING AMERICA, IT'S IMPORTANT TO HAVE VARYING POLITICAL POINTS OF VIEW. **EFFECTIVE DIVERSIFICATION**, matters.

TODAY'S MOST WANTED ARTICLES. FACTS ON FILE **Make an Impact.**

Intelligence Report story BRIEFING

ON Founder of **THE** POSITIVE Faith Religion,

((("HEAVEN ON EARTH EDUCATOR")))

Not The Same Old Song And Dance ⊙

FAIR & BALANCED, EQUAL TIME ANYONE ?

Founder Cites A moral obligation

with **MERGER** Project Restart !

A POSITIVE MIND, is A TERRIBLE THING TO WASTE.

=== PREFACE ===

"I GURU UP ON Religion AND politics."

PACKAGE FOR **When Hell Turned to Heaven**

with PROPOSED REFORMS *That Will Blow You Away!*

defining mission a must read

A PROMISE FULFILLED

DELIVERS.

where to begin →

STEP BY STEP, *A Whole New*

Constitutional freedom *Phenomenon.*

"A Hidden World Discovery Kit

For THIS Voice of the Voiceless, *is*

The 'Real Day The Earth Stood Still ..

Answers to mysterious

End of an age, Prophecy Fulfilled:"

PREFACE (---TINUED)

THIS BOOK'S CONTENTS ARE BASED ON
THE OVER-ALL POSITIVE SCHOOL OF THOUGHT
THAT YOU WERE NEVER ALLOWED TO ATTEND.
FOR THOSE OF YOU THAT
HAVE ALWAYS FELT THAT LIFE IS
UN-FAIR
THIS HERE BOOK MAKES A SERIOUS
EFFORT TO EVEN THE SCORE.
YOUR PRAYERS ANSWERED .

'A BOOK OF TRICKEL DOWN INTELLIGENCE'
WRITTEN BY YOURS TRULY,
LARRY MICHAEL TORREZ = A.K.A. = DR. SUNDAY.
AUTHOR'S POLITICAL PERSUASION; CONNECTING THE DOTS ! FOR THE MOST
PART, IS LIKE THAT OF BEING A 'NO WOODEN NICKLES TAKING, LAST
OF THE MOHICANS 'COMPASSIONATE' FISCAL CONSERVATIVE;
OR A CAPITALIST WHO BELIEVES WE CAN 'ALL CAPITALIZE
TOGETHER. --- AND WHEN SEN. HARRY REID FINDS OUT THAT
I'M A CONSERVATIVE HISPANIC!
(R.E.M. SONG)
♪ IT'S THE END OF THE WORLD AS WE KNOW IT. ♫

Where There's A ⒼⓄⒹ All Mighty Will,

We Are All Connected !

The Sharper Edge
WINNING A WAR OF WORDS
" LET THE OPPOSITIONS CASUALTIES BE THAT OF BRUISED EGO'S."

NATIONWIDE
programing
PLAN ON RECORD-BREAKING TELEVISION!

YOURS TRULY, a politicial 101 Justice FACTORY

takes center stage

Scripture
`THE WILL

According to
personal
RESPONSIBILITY !

BOOK STATEMENTS **Just Listen To What He's Saying on –**

* UN- EMPLOYMENT PROBLEMS *THE FEDERAL BUDGET DEFICIT,

*HEALTH-CARE. *ABORTION. *CRIME & PREVENTION.

ETC-ETC-ETC-ETC-ETC-ETC-ETC-ETC-ETC-ETC-ETC-ETC-ETC-ETC-ETC-ETC-

(1982) YES! "THE WORLD IS A STAGE" AND OR, LIFE IS
NOTHING BUT A P-L-A-Y ON WORLDS--- OR A WORDS.

AUTHOR'S UP-DATE: IT'S ALL KIND OF LIKE ONE BIG REAL LIFE
MOVIE GOING ON OUT THERE; AND I HAVE TO ADMIT
FROM TIME TO TIME —I SLEPT THRU IT.

In my words PAGE 7.

EXCERPTS FROM BOOK, TODAY 'I' MUST CONFESS
BY DR.SUNDAY
PRESIDENTS DAY, FEB.21st,2011

DOES YOUR DEMOCRATIZED - OPINIONATED - VOTE COUNT? MINE DIDN'T!
SO WHY GO AFTER A BUNCH OF POLITICAL SPAWNING MINNOWS, WHEN YOU
CAN TAKE ON THE BIG FISH... (TIME-LINE) 1983: NOTORIOUS FOR
ANSWERING LETTERS FROM COMMON FOLK PEOPLE LIKE MYSELF, I WROTE
TO PRESIDENT REAGAN, IN REFERENCE TO THE EFFECTS OF THE OVER-ALL
"GLAMORIZATION' AND ACCESS TO DRUGS IN THE MOTION PICTURE INDUSTRY
- AND HE NEVER WROTE BACK TO THANK ME...(TIME-LINE) EASTER 1989:
PRESIDENT GEORGE BUSH SR. 'I SENT HIM THIS PROPOSAL FROM
YOURS TRULY, BOOK PAGE 54. - NEVER - EVER - NEVER - LEGALIZE
DRUGS! LEGALIZE HARD CORE, CARD CARRYING DRUG ADDICTS, IN A
CONTROLLED ATTMOSPHERE, AND TAKE A REAL BITE OUT OF CRIME.
'NO MORE CODDLING'. FAR TO MANY INNOCENT VICTIMS HAVE BEEN
ROBBED, BEATEN, OR KILLED; TO APPEASE THEIR HABITS. NEEDLESS
TO SAY DRUG CARTEL! INCESSANTLY WHY MUST SELF-SERVING CLIFF
JUMPING WASTED LIFE, HOLD PRIORTY OVER RESPECTABLE?
RESTORATIVELY A KINDER, GENTLER, DRUG CARTEL... THANK YOU.
LETTERS TO PRESIDENT GEORGE (W) BUSH. - STATEMENT ON
AFGHANISTAN YES! IRAQ NO! KILL WEAPONS OF MASS-DISTRUCTION
= NOT PEOPLE... PRESIDENT OBAMA. (3) LETTERS. - 1 TO BECOME
HIS NEW FAITH BASED PREACHING MINISTER!!! MAYBE HE DIDN'T ANSWER
ME BECAUSE I TOLD HIM, FROM TIME TO TIME I COULD ATLEAST PASS
FOR BEING A BLUE DOG DEMOCRAT! WHAT'S THERE NOT TO LIKE ABOUT
THIS RELATIONSHIP. - 2 LEFT-HANDED CHI-TOWN SOUTH SIDER SPORTS
FAN 1/2 BREEDS, ONE BLACK&WHITE THE OTHER HISPANIC&WHITE, WE
COULD HAVE GOT TOGETHER AND TALKED ABOUT OUR INNER WHITE-BOY
ATTRIBUTES! FIRST AND FOREMOST I, WOULD HAVE TURNED HIM ON TO
MY BOOK PAGE 50! HIS PRAYERS ANSWERED WITH MY JUSTIFIABLE SLAM
DUNK ON THE EMPLOYMENT "COMPETITIONS" FINEST HOUR (TIME-LINE)
1985, PROPOSAL... O'WELL MAYBE I SHOULD HAVE WROTE TO HIS WIFE
MICHELLE, INSTEAD? I'M ALSO BIG ON GROWING VEGY GARDENS AND
GIVING ALOT OF THAT STUFF AWAY. SHE'S DONE GREAT BY WAY OF
"SUGGESTING" TO PEOPLE TO EXERCISE, WATCH ONE'S SALT INTAKE,
ALONG WITH "SOCIET'L CONSCIOUSNESS" TOWARDS RESTAURANT LARGE
PORTIONS, ETC. JUST THE SAME SHE'D BE WELCOME TO READ AND
ENDORSE MY BOOK PAGE 81, ON THAT SUBJECT .. SIGNED YOURS TRULY,
KING FISH...

C H R O N I C L E S
HIGHLIGHT
WE'RE NOT
GONNA TAKE IT Anymore
BEGINS HERE!

FINALLY A LOBBYIST FOR GOD.

Celebrate America

There's a good chance they're going to recognize him this year

Based on Notebooks 'Plan for Prosperity'

As Book lovers gear up for sale —— PAGE 8

"Stop this cover-up!"

FOR THE RECORD Once Upon A Time,

(WILL REMAIN Anonymous)

ALL THE YEARS OF COVER-UP!

Who Knew What, and When?

Pardons DESIGN To Rule.

Political GUARANTEE, Talk show host,

NATION-WIDE

Letters to the Editor ETC,

THAT NEVER GOT ANY RESPONSE.

Memory Lane ➡

Inside today, There comes a TIME in **LIFE** when you've got to Reader's Digest **Newsweek** AND accept a few things.

The Legend Lives On... (PRIORITIZED) .....

.. YOURS TRULY STATEMENTS, TAKEN FROM THIS AN INITIAL 300+ PAGE, 30 YEARS IN THE MAKING, BOOK OF CHAPTERIZED ESSAYS. AUTHOR'S NOTE: OVER THE YEARS APPROXIMATELY 6, OF THESE ESSAYS WERE PUBLISHED BY THE LOCAL NEWS PAPER...

"Facing Up to Reality"

Open Minded Talk, WHAT IS REALITY?

REALITY IS THAT OF AN INDIVIDUAL PERCEPTION! EXAMPLES:
"TO SOME THE GLASS IS HALF-FULL, TO OTHERS IT'S HALF-EMPTY.
ONE MAN'S TRASH IS ANOTHER MAN'S TREASURE.,
ONE MAN'S ECONOMIC CEILING IS ANOTHER MAN'S FLOOR."
THERE'S A PARTICULAR ORDER OF RELIGIOUS EXTREMIST THAT ARE REFERRED TO BY THE
ROMAN CATHOLIC CHURCH AS 'OPUS DEI. — IN THIS MAN'S RELIGION WE REFER TO OUR
RELIGIOUS EXTREMIST AS — SIGNED YOURS TRULY, —

'MAKE MY DAY'...

TAKING STOCK OF statements put on paper
"INVISIBLE GUIDING Art with a
purpose **or** *divine inspiration.*"
Tru calling- **Inking out** A SPIRITUALLY MOTIVATED
written OPINION COMMENTARY takes time to write
CAPITALIZE ON Time Well Spent Serving Your Needs.

Creative writing is new course at PAGE 9

EVIDENCE OF ANSWERS TO
PERSISTENT PRAYER UNLIMITED

.... BOOK *Contents* ....

• **Atrocities of** Democracy -EDITED **chapters on:**

• Intro-**The** LEGEND Of ANYWHERE **but Here** FREE Speech!
of presentation, "**Let freedom truly reign.**"

War & 'Peace' chapter :

long on substance, short on words. PAGES 12 THRU 22.....

(New age) CHAPTER Religious Science, AUTHORIZED BY GOD!

The book A PRODUCT OF A SUPERCONNECTED

MAN, AND HIS GOD ! PAGES 23 THRU 46.

• "That CHAPTER was the week that was". PAGE 47, AND THRU OUT REST OF BOOK:

• *Crime & Punishment* chapter PAGE 57,

United Against Crime Searching For Closure

PAGES THRU U.S.A. NATIONWIDE **Gunman** go **on rampage**

send a **Rapid Fire** *"Spiritual Awakening"* message

Closure to page 64, *Don't you just wish we could—*

```
IF TUFF GUYS DON'T DANCE, THEN WHY READ THEM
THEIR CARMON MIRANDA, RIGHTS? (( 2009 ))
LACKING ANY INDICATORS! - AS A SOCIETY WE'VE
GONE FROM REFERRING TO TERRORIST, TO BEING LOOKED
UPON AS ENEMY COMBATANTS, TO NOW BEING LOOKED UPON
AS ♫ MIDNIGHT AT THE OASIS—'NOT SO
FRIENDLY! PROSECUTION REST.
```
I'M, LIKE SCARED *NOW.*

The Birds & The Bees chapter PAGES 65 THRU

74. *foresight* Better Homes & Gardens.

(((SPORTING NEWS SECTION: PAGES 75 TO 77)))

Professor's challenge is teaching
TOMORROW IN *Education* TODAY

WANTED

New leader, new nation, new world ! →

Big Read

book

answers to

"Peace On Earth Sale"

" GO WHERE NO MAN HAS EVER GONE BEFORE ???

AUTHOR'S NOTE: IF THE DEVIL, OR A

(WASHINGTON THINK TANK AFFILIATE;)

WERE TO OFFER ME, 1 BILLION DOLLARS TO MAKE

ME, FORGET THAT I, EVER WROTE

OR EVEN TRIED TO PROMOTE THIS BOOK ! ?

--- THEN ALL I GOT TO SAY IS

LADIES AND GENTLEMAN,

WELCOME TO THE ORIGIN OF HEAVEN ON EARTH ;

'THY WILL BE DONE "...

2010 FRIAR-FLYER *Discovery Kit* MAY-DAY 2010

Answers to THE POSITIVE Faith Religion.

"where to begin" COLE MINE TRAGEDY, OIL RIG DISASTER, TORNADOS???

MAY-DAY-YEAR   = NEGITIVE RAIN = NEGITIVE REIGN:

2012, IS NOW 24/7 - NATION-WIDE GUNMEN GONE WILD, ETC. EARTHQUAKES, FLOODS, VOLCANOES, POLITICAL LEADERS AND SPORTS FIGURES MORALLY FALLING FROM GRACE; RELIGIOUS PEDOPILES ETC. WAR ESCALATION, POLITICS AS UN-USUAL, ALONG WITH THREATENING POLITICAL PROTESTERS RUN AMUCK! NORMALCY ANYONE? ARMAGEDDON TO YOU YET!?

"" YOU NEED ME. "" SIGNED: YOURS TRULY, THE ANTI-CHRIST.

"END OF DAZE, METER IS RUNNING / HIS TIME IS NOW"!!!

SIGNED: OFFICIAL ✓ 'NEGATIVE SPIRIT BUSTER.

Spiritual Awakening message A wake-up call Exhibit.

··· SO WHO'S THE DEVIL? "THE NEGATIVE SPIRIT" 'INSTIGATOR OF EARTHLY HELL!·····
=EVIL= WORKING THRU MAN, ALONG WITH ONE'S LARGE SCALE ENVIRONMENT.
INTHAT, GLOBAL CATASTROPHES ARE AN ACT OF A.K.A. godZILLA. —EXAMPLE HAITI 2010:
2/3 OF THE PEOPLE THERE ARE INTO VOODOO, AND THE OTHER 1/3 ARE INTO VOODOO ECONOMICS... "DEVIL IN THE DETAILS"? IS MORE LIKE WRITTEN BY MAN, NEGATIVELY INSPIRED BY THE DEVIL; FOUND IN 'ANY AVAILABLE LITERATURE, OR MATERIAL THAT WARRANTS, QR PROMOTES THE 'INSTIGATION OF NEGATIVITY, DISCRIMINATION, HATRED OF, OR HARM TOWARDS OTHERS".
···

'THE SPAGHETTISBERG ADDRESS' : FEBRUARY 14th, 2011

THIS HERE BEING THE "VERBAL, AND OR LITERARY" SAINT VALENTINE'S DAY MASSACRE. 'THIS COMPUTER IS MY SWORD BECAUSE THERE'S ONLY ONE LORD, AND MASTER... RELIGIOUSLY SPEAKING, I KNOW EVERYBODY'S LOOKING FOR RIG---ATONI! - BUT I'M THE REAL ANGEL HAIR, MANICOTTI THAT YOU NEED TO BE DEALING WITH. PERSONALLY I'M FETACHINI UP WITH ALL THOSE PHONY DEMOCRACY PREACHING IM-PASTA-S ANTI-PASTA, CONDEMN'ERS; SOMEDAY THEIR ALL GOING TO REGETA ALL THIS ORZO THEY SAY! 'SO ALL I'M ASKING YOU TO DO IS TO USE YOUR NOODLE AND ROTELLE ON THE ONE'S THAT ARE STELLINE DEMOCRACY FROM YOU! OBVIOUSLY EVERYBODY KNEW I'D SPEAK A STRANGE LANGUAGE, BEING A GENTILE "NATURED" REVOLUTIONARY ROBOT; AND ARE THEY IN FOR A SUPRISE WHEN THEY EXAMINE ME, AND FIND OUT THAT MY DANDRUFF ISN'T REALLY COMPUTER CHIPS AFTER ALL; FOR SHURE BY THEN MY NAME WILL 'ALSO BECOME A UNIVERSAL 'CUSS WORD.
(PARALLELS ANYONE!)

IN THEIR OWN NATIVE DIALECT, THE 'ASIAN PEOPLE HAVE ALWAYS REFERRED TO ME AS (OSSHOLE;) AND THE 'HISPANIC PEOPLE HAVE ALWAYS REFERRED TO ME AS (COWBOY-RONE.) A PENNE FOR YOUR THOUGHTS?

'Life' according to (New-age) Catechism Lessons.

What's INSIDE **First we listen,**

written OPINION COMMENTARY **Rewriting Life Stories**

On pages of
God's Holy Word **GOD** is **THE'**...

READINGS FOR REASONING

How tha story unfolded

🎼 Give'em some of that <u>new-time</u> religion 🎼 PAGE 11.

IN READING THIS GRASSROOTS MANUSCRIPT
ON ALL RELIGIOUSLY EDITED PAGES OF THIS HERE
BOOK; THIS WORD "THE" IS ALWAYS IN DIRECT,
OR INDIRECT REFERENCE TO GOD. THIS WORD "THA"
IS ALWAYS IN DIRECT, OR INDIRECT REFERENCE TO
MAN.EXAMPLE: WITH POSITIVE SPIRIT INTACT WE
ARE "THA" LITTLE EXTENSIONS FROM "THE" BIG

EXTENDER, AS OPPOSE TO "THE" LITTLE
EXTENSIONS, OR LITTLE ~~gods~~. WE ARE "THA"
SO TO SPEAK ANTS, AND GOD, IS "THE"
GI---ANT' ALL ONE BIG FAMILY;
INTHAT TO BE 'A RELIGIOUSLY ACTIVATED
CARD CARRYING MEMBER OF THA "TRUE"
FAMILY OF GOD; THERE IS 'NO
ETHNICAL DIFFERENCES AMONG MAN---KIND...

... And They Lived Happily Ever After."

"Peace On Earth" 2011, *WRITING LIKE THERE'S NO*
TOMORROW. Democracy **Tha Promised Land?**

'War & Peace'
Tha Next Chapter

AMAZING VIEWS

News, notes, quips & quotes

Observations, confessions and revelations

Attention to detail

BY
THE
BOOK

There's never been a better time to

Live —————— and learn.

FRIAR FLIER
Wit & Wisdom :

THIS HERE STORY IS ABOUT THIS `PRIORITIZED, MORALLY
SAMSONIAN — MAN AND HIS — GOD,
TAKING ON ALL OF AL-QAIDA.

((((THA <u>POSITIVE</u> RESULTS ARE IN))))

"THEY `HAVEN'T GOT A <u>PRAYER</u>".

unforgettable images

Letters to the Editor RENO GAZETTE-JOURNAL

THANK YOU KINDLY FOR PUTTING THA FLAG IN NEWS PRINT, THIS IS A GREAT SERVICE TO THA COMMUNITY. I NOW DISPLAY THIS PROUDLY IN MY PLACE OF EMPLOYMENT., AS THIS HERE ESSAY is DEDICATED TO ALL THA PEOPLE THAT LOST THEIR LIVES ON (**911**) AND THEIR FAMILIES !

"OBSERVATION **Answers** TO *INSTIGATORS OF HELL*" AANYONE ?` IN AS FAR AS PURSUING THA GUILTY is CONCERN. DON'T LET THA CANDY ASPIRATIONS OF THA PACIFIST HOLD JURY TO THESE NEGATIVE SPIRITED — DEGENERATIVE LOW-LIFERS, WE NEED TO RID THA PLANET OF. THIS WHOLE WEEK HAS BEEN LIKE LIVING IN A REAL LIFE BAD MOVIE TO ME. THUS WAKING UP AND CLICKING OUR SOULS TOGETHER. THERE'S NO PLACE LIKE AMERICA, THERE'S NO PLACE LIKE AMERICA !

"My Fellow Americans" `SOME DAY ALL ONE, GOD BLESS AMERICA. 'Hallelujah'.

Looking to pound home a message.
INTENTIONAL FRIENDLY FIRE ???

`WHAT WAS THAT (TV) COMMENT ABOUT THA FATE OF COMMON FOLK AIRLINE PASSENGERS FLYING IN A HIJACKED PLANE AND HEADING FOR A UNSCHEDULE WHITE HOUSE DROP IN VISIT ?

YOUR CHOICE, BE THIS HERE A DOOMS DAY PORTFOLIO, OR A YOURS TRULY, INSTIGATOR DETERRENT PROPOSAL; FOLLOW-UP IN CRIME & PUNISHMENT CHAPTER FINALLY ...

An expert's prayer

WRITTEN BY MAN 'INSPIRED BY GOD.

NATION-WIDE *Letters to tha Editor* MARCH 2011

THA SEARCH FOR SIGNS OF INTELLIGENT LIFE IN THA UNIVERSE???

= PLEASE FORWARD TO =

DEAR GADHAFI-DUCK, HAPPY EASTER!

'YOUR LIFE IS LIKE THAT OF YOU BEING A CARTOON CHARACTER, YOU CAN'T BE FOR REAL; SO I'M GOING TO REEL YOU IN! FACETIOUS BUGS BUNNY HARE, WITH YOU CAN EAT THIS RAIS'ON! - A WEEK OR SO AGO, ON THA PODIUM YOU MENTIONED SOMETHING ABOUT GOD, BEING ON YOUR SIDE !!!??? "I KNOW GOD, AND WHAT GOD, HAS INSTILLED IN ME IS THAT, THA INSTIGATION OF WAR 'IS MANS GREATEST OF SIN! THOU SHELT NOT — INSTIGATE KILL, PERIOD"!

DANGLING CARROT ROUTINE ANYONE? THEREFORE REPENT: CALL FOR A PEACE TRUCE AND SPREAD THA sustainable" WEALTH AMONG ALL THA PEOPLES OF LIBYA.

"FORMULA FOR AN OVERALL MID-EAST UPHEAVAL,ETC"!

♫ THIS LAND IS YOUR LAND, THIS LAND IS OUR LAND; END GAME? BECOME A HERO IN THE EYES OF GOD! - OR GRAB YOURSELF A DESIGNERS SUITCASE FULL OF MONEY - MAN'UP, AND LET THA FASHION POLICE ESCORT YOU OUT OF TOWN; DO A CAREER MAKEOVER AND START YOURSELF A BRAND NEW CAREER AS A FASHION RUNWAY CONSULTANT, IN UPSTARTING YOUR OWN LINE OF APPAREL...

¢¢¢ IRRELIGIOUS LEADERSHIP ANYONE? "FOR THA TRUE LOVE OF GOD" LET THERE BE STRENGTH IN NUMBERS! PEACEFUL EVOLUTION, REVOLUTION IS THA SOLUTION, TO BE FREE OF MENTAL POLUTION; AMEN.¢¢¢

SIGNED: WHAT WOULD ANTI-JESUS DO? YOU GOT IT BABE! THA EASTER BUNNY COMETH...

"" WINNING""

♫ experiences a renaissance

THEME OF PAGE 12 SERIES, AND OR CHAPTER SONG!

HEAVEN'S BELLS, IF YOU'RE <u>EVIL</u> YOU'RE - 'NO - FRIEND OF MINE.

Get what you pay for

MARCH-2011

'HELPING PEOPLE THAT ARE BEING PHYSICALLY SLAUGHTERED (VERSUS)
FINANCIALLY; ONE HAND WASHES THA OTHER. RIGHT TO THA POINT CRISIS
SOLVING! THEREFORE "ASK NOT WHAT YOUR COUNTRY CAN DO FOR YOU, BUT
WHAT YOU CAN DO FOR YOUR COUNTRY" IN LIBYA, THA TOWNIES PAY 40¢ A
GALLON FOR GAS; SO LET'S MAKE A DEAL WITH THEM BY WAY OF ARMING THA
REBELS AND AT THA SAME TIME OFFERING THEM 50¢ A GALLON FOR GAS, INTHAT
HAVING GUIDO AND THA BOY'S SET UP A TRANSPORT SHOP IN THA GOOD OL' U.S.
OF A. - FOR A $1.00 A GALLON! EVERYTHING'S POSSIBLE; THUS COMPETITIONS
FINEST HOUR. 'FREEDOM ISN'T FREE' WE COULD ALSO PRI-OPEN IRAQ'S TOWNIE
MOTHER LOAD FOR A KICKER! ALL IN ALL BRINGING BACK DEAD AND BURIED EX-
PRESSIONS LIKE - I'VE GOT MONEY I AIN'T SPENT YET; LET'S GO CRUISING.
ETC. ETC. IN CONCLUSION, DRIVING A STAKE THRU THA HEART OF THIS MONSTER

INFLATION...

THIS HERE PETROL CRISIS SO COSTLY THAT MADAGASCAR, HAS NOW BEEN
RE-NAMED 'MAD I CAN'T AFFORD ANYMORE GAS IN MY CAR'...

The book January 1, 2010

ACCESSING THA FUTURE *Leadership Solutions,* BY WAY OF THA
PERTINENT PRIORITIES OF A PROMETHEAN
PROMULGATOR, OR A PERSPICIOUS PUPPET-PUNDIT,
ON THA PODIUM. "STAY THIRSTY MY FRIENDS!"

Letters to tha Editor CONNECTING THA DOTS?
IN REFERENCE TO THA CHRISTMAS DAY,
FRUIT OF THA 'BOOM' TERRORIST BOMBER!

EVER SINCE THAT INCIDENT HAPPENED; WHY IS IT THAT 'I SEEM
TO BE THA ONLY ONE ASKING THA QUESTION OF HOW DID HE MANAGE
TO GET THAT PARTICULAR SEAT ON THA AIRPLANE THAT WAS DIRECTLY
OVER THA MAJOR FUEL TANKS? TALK ABOUT HITTING THA LOTTERY!
WHAT DID HE DO, CHARM THA SOX OFF SOME FASHION POLICE TICKET
AGENT? BESIDES A 'LIGITIMATE TRAVELER WITHOUT LUGGAGE WOULD HAVE
NATURALLY REQUESTED FOR A SEAT UP FRONT FOR A QUICK EXIT STRATEGY!
RED FLAG LAUNDRY LIST OF CONSPIRACY ANYONE? SO WHAT'S NEXT, A
BRA TOTING DOLLY PARTON TYPE, JIHADIST? AUTHOR'S NOTE: AHA FOR
THA GOOD OLD DAYS! SOMEDAY ENEMY COMBATANT, IS GOING TO KICK IN...

IN CONCLUSION= THA KORAN ACCORDING TO: A RACIST TERRORIST, TOWARDS
(INFIDELS! ETC.) LITERATELY INSPIRED BY THA NOT SO GREAT SATAN!
(VERSUS) YOURS TRULY, THA NEW-AGE BIBLICAL EDITING SAVIOUR OF,
'LOVE THY NEIGHBOR' THUS ALL GOD'S CHILDREN EXPRESS...

Tha Look-Ahead Factor *That Won't Go Away*

War *Tha greatest of sin* (versus)

When Words Are tha Best Weapon:

"<u>Truth</u>" IS MORE POWERFUL THAN ANY MAN MADE BOOMB OR NUCLEAR DEVICE, BECAUSE WHEN THA OPPOSITION READS THIS BOOK - 'BOY ARE THEY GOING TO EXPLODE !

Will those who expose fraud in science be tomorrow's heroes?

Reality Check THA HIGH PRIORITIES OF THIS MAN'S RELIGION, FOCUSES ON THIS BOOK'S `THOU SHELT NOT — INSTIGATE — KILL' FACTOR.., ALONG WITH (iNiTiAL) PAGE 51, **on** CREED.

WHEREAS `THIS iS HOW ONE BEHAVIORALLY LEGITIMATIZES, iN HAVING A REALISTIC PRAYER RAPOR **WITH** God. *Amen*.

BEHIND 'tha LINES 🦁 THA page 12½ *MENU OF A*

ARMAGETTING AESTLESS LION. Note,

Political LION PARTY Founder OR, CAT-MAN-DUE.

Destination tha world stage defining mission a must read.

Kuwait 1991 **STEPPIN' OUT PACKAGE** History Shorts **is so yesterday.**

Countdown to JUSTICE TIME Giving Back What Was Taken

YOU'VE GOT NATIONAL LETTERS TO Tha EDITOR MAIL.

SAFEKEEPING DEMOCRACY - ? — Great History *CHALLENGES* BY YOURS TRULY:

"TO MAKE HiM THiNK, iS TO MAKE HiM BLiNK".→

Gulf showdown (((PREDICTION)))

FROM BAGHDAD TO BAGHLADY, OR
BAATH PARTY TAKES A SHOWER !

DEAR SADDAM HUSSEIN; just Kuwait

AND YOU'LL BE CAUGHT BETWEEN

IRAQ AND A HARD PLACE ! 'message GET OUT OF KUWAIT.

Iraq 1991, ThaMessage that Once Was, Is Not Forgotten!' RIPE FOR
JUDGEMENT
EXTRA-LIFE
return.
"UPON THEIR SURRENDER! GO IN THERE AND
(((((((((((((((arrest SADDAM HUSSEIN.))))))))))))))))

FOR GRANDIOSE POLUTION., WAR CRIMES ETC."

'leadership Failure' Life of A terrorists rolls on.

Iraq Dec.02., "Peace On Earth"—T-SHIRT-SALE

Alternative What's a life worth? EPA $3.7 million.

♯ I'M LOOK'EN AT THA MAN IN THA MEDIA ♯

is SADDAM Relocating WITH exile ?

When All Else Fails

OPERATION IRAQI FREEDOM

scholars dis=cuss history as it unfolds

Written in early NOVEMBER 2003

Iraq -8- months LATER

A look at U.S. deaths in Iraq

CONTEMPLATING LONGEVITY OF MISSION TO DIE FOR! A YANKEE COME HOME EXIT STRATEGY, ANYONE? **Prediction'** "NO MATTER IF WE LEAVE **Iraq** 10 DAYS FROM NOW, OR 10 YEARS., NO SOONER DO WE EXIT AND CIVIL WAR WILL BREAK-OUT IN A HEART-BEAT!" LIKEWISE **Prediction'** **ON** AFGHANISTAN, **Same Old story-different day!** "MY COMEDY CLUB IMPERSONATION OF" YA KNOW YA COULD BE A RED-NECK A-RAB, IF YOU'RE DENYING WOMEN THEIR BASIC EQUAL RIGHTS. **OR found in** TRANSLATION!

2002 Groundbreaking News

comedy club: DADDY, WHAT'S GROUNDHOG DAY? "THAT'S WHEN OSAMA BIN LADEN COMES OUT OF HIS CAVE, AND IF HE SEES HIS SHADOW — THAT MEANS WE'VE GOT 6 MORE WEEKS OF TERRORISM!". SIGNED: HOOSIER DADDY

March 25, 2004

ON BOMBING SUSPECT: IRRELIGIOUS TRICKS OF THA TRADE

This sounds familiar. "HE WAS TOLD OF A PROMISED HEAVENLY ASCENSION BY WAY OF GETTING TO ROLL IN THA HAY WITH SOME 72 VIRGINS., GIVE OR TAKE A FEW EXPERIENCED PORN STARS. **NOTICE IS HEREBY GIVEN** *Now, this is one big 'Gotcha'* THA REVEALING OF THA GOSPEL ACCORDING TO A SEX-MANIAC."

WHAT THEY SAY **ABOUT cartoon** storytelling
DISCLOSURE   FEBRUARY 2006

Great leaders must be thick-skinned

In tha news, in reference to tha cartoons about tha Prophet Muhammad: Tha one about tha bomb is disrespectful, and I can understand protest, but not riot! I thought tha one about all tha virgins was very funny. Fact is, whenever one lies about one's religion (and/or any religion) to achieve an objective, they should be subject to open criticism! In retrospect, tha real shame within is tha lie that defaced one's religion in tha first place.

Besides, history will tell you that all tha great leaders were thick-skinned. Example: "Tha King David philosophy of sticks and stones will break my bones, but words will never hurt me!"

BY YOURS TRULY, A.K.A. DR. SUNDAY

LIFE IN THESE UNITED STATES.'

"REAL"

VALEDICTORIAN OF **StreetSmart Paper Prison** Writer,   FACTS

Looking to pound home a message   OF

LIFE'.

(((SUPER NICE VS. SUPER SMART))). (VOTE YES ON NUCLEAR ARSENAL '

Taking in Knowledge NOW & FOREVER

EVEN IF THERE WERE "Peace On Earth FOR THA NEXT 50 YEARS," IN AS FAR AS THA BULK OF PRIORITIES GO; I WOULD NEVER PREPONDERANTLY UNDER-BUDGET OUR ARMED FORCES!" `FACT IS NO MATTER HOW GOD LOVING, AND MORALLY COMMITED ONE IS PERSONALLY! THERE'S ALWAYS SOME UN-JUSTIFIABLE MORALLY WEAK MINDED, `DEVIL PROVOKED INDIVIDUAL, OR ORGANIZATION OUT THERE THAT YOU JUST CAN'T TRUST ETC.

IMAGINATION ADVENTURE

THOUGHTS OF LIVING IN PARADISE? EVEN IF WE WERE ALL GLOBALLY OF THA SAME EXACT COLORFUL ETHNIC BACKROUND, AND SACRED COW RELIGION., JUST WHEN YOU THOUGHT EVERYTHING WAS COPACETIC. FOR STARTERS, EVENTUALLY SOME PREEMINENT POLITICAN, WOULD GO FORTH AND DECLARE A ETHNICALLY CLEANSING TYPE CIVIL WAR, ON THA STUPID. INCIPENTLY THA FIRST VERBAL SHOTS TAKEN IN THIS WAR WOULD BE— "IT'S THA ECONOMY STUPID." — PAGE 16 —

Live from tha cemetery ¡ see Dead people."

"ERADICATION - HERE'S LOOKING AT YOU AL-QAIDA!" ON 911, HAD I BEEN THA COMMANDER IN CHIEF, THA RIGHT WAY TO HAVE GONE INTO AN UNINFORMED AFGHANISTAN, SHOULD HAVE BEEN BY WAY OF A D-DAY SURPRISE! — WE COULD HAVE GIVEN THA PAKISTANI PRESIDENT, A 45 MINUTE NOTICE $., AND BIN LADEN, WOULD HAVE BEEN TOAST. — LIKE-WISE WITH SADDAM HUSSEIN, FROM THA VERY ANTICIPATION OF THIS WAR, I WOULD HAVE SENT IN A DOUBLE AGENT MAFIA STYLE HIT-MAN, TO TAKE CARE OF HIM. SIGNED: BY ALL OF THIS WAR'S COLLATERAL DAMAGE GHOST.

TAKE THEM DEEP 'MORALLY SPEAKING IN A WAR, LIFE + DEATH IS A NUMBERS GAME. →

Wing Commander WARFIGHTING ESSAY CONTEST

<u>VISION</u> Even Without A Flea Collar, *Written by* THA BARKING ANGEL *with* THA DOGMA, THAT HAS THA REAL BITE TO IT. **Page** *and moment is frozen in time.*

THE BOOK | page 2B, OR NOT 2B.   PAGE 17

Millions spent to influence Congress

— Yeah, AND I'M JUST TRYING TO GET MY .2¢, WORTH IN!

CAMALOT, OR   CAMEL-LOT REGIME?

Everything to Everyone

((("FROG HAS SPOKEN")))

11/1/06

Righteously Combating madness

EXIT STRATEGY ? 3 YEARS OF ON going IRAQI MILITARY BASIC TRAINING WITHOUT ANY STABILITY, TELLS YOU THAT THA REAL SOCIETAL BASIC TRAINING THEY NEED TO BE TAUGHT OVER THERE IS IN THA GOD LOVING, BROTHERHOOD OF MAN. JJ THIS IS HOW LIFE SHOULD BE JJ. ✳ LIVING IN A COUNTRY (USA) THAT CARRIES SO MUCH EMPHASIS ON ATTAINING A QUALITY EDUCATION! "WHEREAS THA EDUCATIONAL PRIORITY HERE IS OBVIOUSLY THA ONE YOU CAN'T CHEAT YOUR WAY THROUGH SCHOOL ON!" (DISSECTING ANALYSIS.) THEREFORE EVEN IF YOUR GOD IS A FROG.., THA FROG WANTS YOU TO BEHAVE YOURSELF. "FROG HAS SPOKEN." I TOAD YOU SO!"

—— WHAT EVER THIS IS GOING TO TAKE ——

═══════ REFORM PLAN. ═══════

THA SEARCH FOR SIGNS OF INTELLIGENT LIFE IN THA UNIVERSE?

Yes, You Can...

THA real' SPIN STOPS HERE!

FEBRUARY 2006

OPINION on Port WHINNING CONTROVERSY

"JUST ANOTHER TROJAN HORSE REPLAY WAITING TO HAPPEN!" HAVING UNITED ARAB EMIRATES TO ASSUME CONTROL OF OPERATIONS AT SIX MAJOR AMERICAN PORTS — IS LIKE HIRING THA FOX TO GUARD THA CHICKEN COOP — FOR THA MOST PART WITH US BEING OVER THERE IN THESE ISLAMIC COUNTRYS, TO THEM IT'S EQUIVALENT TO THA KU KLUX KLAN, MOVING INTO A LARGE BLACK AMERICAN COMMUNITY, AND TRYING TO RUN THEIR AFFAIRS., 'GET REAL, THEY HATE US! HOW SOON DO WE FORGET ABOUT THA BARRACKS BOMBING IN FRIENDLY SAUDI ARABIA., ALONG WITH THA BOMBING OF THA COLE IN YEMEN! PERSONALLY SPEAKING, UNTIL THEY GET INTELLECTUAL WIND OF, WHO'S SIDE IS GOD ON? GOD, IS ON THA SIDE OF ALL THA POSITIVE DEED DOING MELIORISTIC! HOORAY FOR OUR SIDE."

Sample A Touch of Heaven
Climb aboard

PAGE 17½

LET tha POWER of 'Truth', BE THA SALVATION OF ANGER AND FRUSTRATION MORE POWERFUL THAN A NUCLEAR WAR HEAD, OR ARMY OF TERRORIST, THA LESSON OF A LIFE TIME." The MESSAGE HEARD."

FREE Editorial PRESS

FEBRUARY 2006   Internet post by Al-Qaida ASSOCIATED PRESS

VERSUS BOGUS RHETORIC Al-Qaida's INSPIRED WORD".

vows more attacks

There are more like-them who are racing toward martyrdom and eager to fight tha enemies of God.'

Your guide to A kinder, gentler judgment day

(ANSWERS TO POSITIVE WORLD- INFORMATION to general public.)

BJORN AND RAISED, I SALUTE MY COUNTRY USA., IN REGARDS TO DECEMBER 26TH, 2004. FOR WHEN A VAST MUSLIM REGION GOT HIT BY A DEVASTING TSUNAMI., TO THA RESCUE WE RESPONDED WITH BIG TIME ECONOMICAL SUPPORT, ETC! HUMBLING IN REALITY, BY WAY OF REVICTUALING THY BRETHREN, I LOVE THA SMELL OF HONOR THY NEIGHBOR IN THA MORNING! 'THEREFORE DID WE JUST BANK ON FOREIGN NEWS MEDIA TO FORETELL OF OUR KINDNESS AND GENEROSITY ? IN OTHER WORDS DO THESE INSURGENTS EVEN HAVE A CLUE WE CAME FORTH WITH THIS KIND OF A NOBEL EFFORT ? FURTHERMORE IF THA USA. DIDN'T INTERVENE IN BOSNIA, THERE WOULD BE NO MUSLIM COMMUNITY THERE., ALONG WITH UPHOLDING THA HISTORIC SOVEREIGNTY OF KUWAIT. (UP-DATED) 'I COULD HAVE STATED SOMETHING ABOUT US HELPING OUT WITH THA EARTH QUAKE VICTIMS IN PAKISTAN. **From hear to eternity** (ANSWERS TO WELCOME TO THA **kinder, gentler** BLESSINGS OF A DEMOCRATIZED CIVILAZATION !"

You are now officially out of excuses.

experience

"HAVING A BEAUTIFUL MIND".

EVER SINCE I'VE BEEN GIVEN THA LOW DOWN ON OSAMA BIN LADEN'S POLITICS, AND HIS REASONS FOR BEING DISCONTENT WITH AMERICA. I CAME TO THA CONCLUSION THAT IN EVERY WAY SHAPE AND FORM, HE LACKED BEING ANY KIND OF A VISIONARY; AS OPPOSE TO BEING DISTRUCTIVE WITH HIS MONEY, HE SHOULD HAVE FORESEEN THA FUTURE AND INVESTED **Big Time** IN AMERICA. THA WORD **DIVERSIFY** SHOULD HAVE BEEN TATTOOED ON HIS FORE-HEAD!

Tell us what you think

SOLUTION

` BECAUSE IN THA FUTURE, PEOPLE LIVING IN THAT REGION <u>IF THEY</u> <u>DON'T</u>, THA REAL WAR WILL BEGIN THA DAY THOSE OIL WELL'S DRY UP.

WALL ST   Like a Pro

"LIFE IS LIKE A BOX OF CHO-COLATE COVERED TURTLES, IN THIS CASE YOU ALWAYS KNOW WHAT YOUR GOING TO GET."

2008 BACK BY POPULAR DEMOND,. A RIGHTEOUS ROLLING STONE, GATHERS NO- Hamas!!

"INSTIGATORS" OF UN-HOLY-LAND., MARTYR-DUMB FAR FROM HEAVEN Ohhh...Yeah! 'tired of being stupid'. Stop, Stop, Stop and Think- DIE ANOTHER DAY. baaaad ideeeeaaa TAKING ON ISRAEL, WITH THOSE 4TH of JULY ROCKETS, AND EXPECTING THEM TO LEAVE TOWN., IS ABOUT AS EQUIVALENT AT BEST TO BEING A MEDIOCRE COLLEGE FOOTBALL TEAM, AND TAKING ON THA CHICAGO BEARS, IN A WINNER TAKE ALL $, STUPER BOWL GAME.

"DON'T TRY THIS AT HOME TAX PAYER'S! 'REWARDING THA HAMAS TERRORIST, 'FOR DOING WRONG' WITH 900 MILLION DOLLARS TO REBUILD A BETTER ARSENAL IS BEYOND ONE'S IMAGINATION! "FEEL LUCKY PUNK."

INTHAT IF YOU HAD ISRAEL'S FIRE POWER YOU'D WIPE THEM OFF THA FACE OF THA EARTH. AS I PREVIOUSLY STATED IN MY BOOK; LET IRAN ETC, RE-BUILD THESE JERK'S INFRASTRUCTURE AND THEY'LL NEVER FIND ENOUGH MONEY TO UP-GRADE THEIR OWN ARSENAL... LIFE IS PSYCHOLOGY--- SIGNED: DR. SUNDAY PAGE 19.

IN BRIEF: THE BIBLE'S VIEWPOINT ON Torture.

NON-ACCEPTABLE WATER-BOARDING IS FOR SURFERS. "ACCORDING TO" WHAT'S DO-ABLE? THA CREATIVE ART OF EXTREME SLEEP DEPRAVATION, IS ADEQUATE OR SA-FISH-ANT...

"Taking your notebook out for a test drive; I LOVE THA SMELL OF REVOLUTION IN THA MORNING!"

USA TODAY - WEDNESDAY, MARCH 31, 2004 - 11A

PAGE 19½

News BRIEF

quotes

" $ "

Studies on Palestinian mothers and children suggest how difficult it is to safely raise children there. "At tha age of 12, children start to look for role models. In tha States you have celebrities and athletes." "In our part of tha world it is tha martyr." everyone tells them their child will go to paradise."

"FOLLOW-UP IN SPORTING NEWS SECTION"

On record 1984 SPORTING NEWS **proposal**

'Americanizing GAMES'
A big league lesson in caring!

(New Age Marketing Program) Tha mission that changed tha world.

with Free Speech PROPOSAL. ←

Letters DEAR NEWS MEDIA, **Tap tha POWER On**

→ WASHINGTON lawmakers

tough Love Letters from Home

"HELL WOULD BE THA PERFECT PLACE TO LIVE WITHOUT ME, BECAUSE THEN YOU, WOULD HAVE NO-BODY LIKE ME, TO QUESTION YOUR JUDGMENT, OR CONSCIOUS."

WASHINGTON SIGNED: WE DON'T NEED ANOTHER HERO

Congratulations, You've Just Been Rejected ..

Then and now Your Life Stories REVISITED

Lobbying tha world For Peace

— ALL THESE WONDERFUL ATTRIBUTES ABOUT LIVING IN A DEMOCRACY, AND SHOULD (((SOMEBODY))) EVER DECIDE TO PRINT WHAT I'VE WRITTEN ABOUT ON ALL OF THIS??? — PRICELESS...

IN THA NEWS : PEACE IN THA MIDEAST ?
THA ONLY WAY THA TWO STATE SOLUTION WOULD
WORK BETWEEN ISRAEL AND THA PALESTINIANS .,
WOULD BE IF YOU MAKE ISRAEL OUR 51ST STATE .,
AND PALESTINE THA STATE OF ALERT. SIGNED :
HOME SCHOOLED BY GOD, I'M ALWAYS RIGHT !.
— YOU KNOW HOW ONE 'GAINS POLITICAL AUTH-
ORITATIVE LEADERSHIP IN THA FATAH PARTY ?
THEY ALL GATHER AROUND IN A ROOM AND TAKE
A LOOK AT ONE ANOTHER, AND 'ONE ONLY STEPS
FORWARD AND SAYS : 'YOU KNOW I THINK I'M,
ALOT MORE FATAH THEN ALL THA REST OF YOU
GUYS! IN THA NEWS : ON THAT NEW OMNIBUS
BILL! I SUPPORT THAT ONE THAT WILL SNIFF
OUT THA POLITICANS THAT ARE TRYING TO INTRODUCE
PORK BILLS 0., I THINK THAT WAS WHAT THEY WERE
TRYING TO SAY ON T.V. ABOUT PORK SNIFFING ?
SO MUCH FOR GUSTATORY MULTI-TASKING WHILE WATCHING THA NEWS.
LET'S SEE., UP NEXT IS THAT ONE ABOUT BULLYING, FOR
$400,000 ! "TO BECOME A GRADUATE OF POPULARITY
SCHOOL-THIS CAN ONLY BE ACHIEVED BY WAY OF ATT-
AINING OTHER PEOPLES RESPECT. — ARE YOU GAME ?
'IN THAT ONE LEARNS THAT FEAR IS CONTRARY TO —
RESPECT., FOR ONE CAN NEVER PHYSICALLY OR
MENTALLY, BEAT RESPECT INTO AN OPPOSITION
— ONLY FEAR 0. 'NOW YOU NO LONGER HAVE TO BE A
FREUD OF THA UN-KNOWN. 'THIS IS CHRIST PEOPLE!,
EARMARKED FOR PROSPERITY; "SHOW ME THAT MONEY".

Heaven Is a Place on Earth sets example

Study: Al-Qaida regroups

AS STATED IN THA NEWS. "NO OPTIONS ARE OFF THA TABLE IN PROTECTING THA AMERICAN PEOPLE!" IF THA good 'OL USA, WANTS TO POLICE THA WORLD TO 9T'S OWN INTRUST IN PLAYING THA PATROLLING ROLL OF good COP, — THEN THRU THA WONDERS OF A FREE SPEACH EXTRAVAGANZA, (TV) `LET ME PLAY THA ROLL OF BAD COP, AS A MORAL AUTHORITATIVE IN YOUR FACE. "NONEXEMPT RELIGIOUS TAX PAYING" LIVE WIRE, CHALLENGING THEIR RECRUITMENT THAT AL-QAIDA, IS NOTING MORE THEN A "SATANIC CULT." `VERBALLY TERRORIZING ALL THOSE LOW-LIFE TYPES, INTO POSITIVE SUBMISSION. SIGNED: CHRISTMAS IN JULY, — JULY 25th, 07'

written OPINION COMMENTARY BY DR. SUNDAY

LETTERS SENT TO RATINGS WAR NETWORKS — ABC NEWS, NBC, CBS, AND FOX ...

Get ready for truth **support**...

Preacher, Political analyst, **puts you in touch :**
`SOUL IS THE AURA OF ONE'S INNER GOODNESS. FOR ONLY TRUE LEADERSHIP WOULD ACCEPT POSITIVE INPUT. THUS DEMOCRACY'S FINENESS HOUR. RETROSPECTIVELY EVERYBODY WANTS TO RULE ♫ THA WORLD. WHEREBY EVERYBODY SHOULD VIA THE POSITIVE, INSTRUMENTING THA REALITY OF GOD'S WORLD.

YOURS TRULY SIGNED,

Freedom at Work — Do SOMETHING ABOUT It —
future is no Kidding matter.

"My Fellow Americans RELIGIOUSLY `PRIORITIZED MORALLY STRONG — Tough Guys Finish FIRST."

This is one heck of a 'What 'They Did for This Summer' story ,. july 2006 Report on HEZBOLLAH:

PAGE 22.

PARTY OF GOD? I KNOW GOD! AND YOU'RE DEFINITELY NO PARTY OF (GOD), HEZBOLLAH. WHEREAS GOD, WAS NOWHERE TO BE FOUND WHEN YOU 'INSTIGATED THIS WARRING UPHEAVAL AGAINST ISRAEL. FAILURES OF NICE SCHOOL! THERE IS NO PLACE FOR RACIAL PREJUDICE, OR HATRED TOWARDS OTHERS IN THIS MANS RELIGION.

WAR AND REMEMBRANCE *Great Getaways* "NO MORE DRAFT."

BUILT TO LAST FOREVER IN THIS COUNTRY. TOURS OF DUTY BY OUR MILITARY IN WAR-TORN IRAQ, OR AFGHANISTAN ETC, SHOULD BE BY WAY OF 'THEIR — INDIVIDUAL-CHOICE BEING 'VOLUNTARY., OR WRITTEN BY A DRAFTED U.S. ARMY VETERAN — AND SHOULD THERE EVER BE A POPULAR WAR, YOU'D NEVER HAVE TO WORRY ABOUT HAVING A DRAFT. II- PUT ME IN COACH, SGT I'M READY TO PLAY! FURTHERMORE TRYING TO PROMOTE DEMOCRACY IN A FOREIGN LAND, WHEN YOU HAVEN'T TESTIFYABLY, PROMOTED IT JUSTIFIABLY, IN YOUR OWN., IS AN INSULT TO ONE'S OWN INTELLIGENCE. This sounds familiar. 'FREEDOM ISN'T-FREE.'STICKER SHOCK! LET THESE HOST COUNTRIES PICK UP THIS DURATIONEL TAB $. 'WE COULD HAVE BETTER WELL-SPENT THA MONEY ON NATION-WIDE HEALTH CARE IN THIS COUNTRY. SIGNED:

Tha LEGEND Of ANYWHERE but Here FREE Speech!

"Peace On Earth"

WRITTEN BY YOURS TRULY, IN 1991:
ANSWERS TO TESTIMONIAL DOCUMENT SIGNING:

Tha Look-Ahead Factor *That Won't Go Away*

Reality Check *screening device for* presidential *candidates.*

(((GLOBALLY SPEAKING))) **When Hell Turned to Heaven!**

Tha Roads Not Taken—'so **Crooks, Creeps and Cons** Will Never Come to Power!'

If you are serious this could be tha MOST IMPORTANT ad you will ever read.

'**Peace**' On Earth, Meet a Sales Counselor Whose First Priority Is You. **Taking in Knowledge NOW & FOREVER —War** PAGE 22½

Tha greatest of sin (**versus**) *YOURS TRULY*, **Gospel Today** Peace Policy, tha meaning of life. I KNOW-WHEREOF-I-SPEAK; WE BY CHOICE ARE EITHER ON THIS HERE PLANET EARTH TO WILL FULLY SERVE ALMIGHTY God DILIGENTLY ., NOT THA CONTRARY. THUS UNIFYING THA REALITY OF Peace On Earth! policy remains firm. *This Certificate* NO MORE WARS!

People from diverse cultures cooperate for understanding.

I HAVE READ, UNDERSTOOD, AND AGREE TO ABIDE BY GOD. sign oath!

name _ _ _ _ _ _ _ _ _ _ _ _ _ Date _ _ _ _ _ _ _

Tha Shots Still Echo
"OPEN SEASON ON COMMON FOLK CITIZENS."!

GO TO *Crime & Punishment* chapter,

Featuring Soul Revival PROPOSAL a must read.

Religious Science
Tha Next Chapter

AMAZING VIEWS
News, notes, quips & quotes
Observations, confessions and revelations

"FREEDOM OF CHOICE, CONVERSION KIT."

MY DEAR BRETHREN,

WORRIED ABOUT COMPETITION?
LET THERE BE NUN!

JUST PREACH `MY GOSPEL, AND GLOBALLY
YOU'LL KEEP ALL YOUR PARISHIONERS!!!

WELCOME TO RELIGIOUS AND POLITICAL SUNDAY SCHOOL:

WHO IS THA DEVIL?
"THAAA NEGITIVE SPIRIT"
'INSTIGATOR OF EARTHLY HELL,

INTHAT GLOBAL CATASTROPHES ARE AN ACT OF A.K.A. godZILLA.

"DEVIL IN THA DETAILS"? WORKING THRU MAN,

IS MORE LIKE REALISTICALLY WRITTEN BY MAN,
INSPIRED BY THA DEVIL;
WHEREAS RESULTS ARE FOUND IN 'ANY AVAILABLE LITERATURE,
OR MATERIAL THAT WARRANTS, OR PROMOTES THA 'INSTIGATION OF
NEGATIVITY, DISCRIMINATION, HATRED OF, OR HARM TOWARDS OTHERS"...

 THIS HERE BOOK IS DEDICATED TO THE ONE AND ONLY,
ALWAYS WAS AND ALWAYS WILL BE, `POSITIVE MIRACLE
WORKING GOD! SIGNED: ALL GOD'S CHILDREN...

Earmarking for education

"CAN YOU SAY THAT THA PRIORITY OF EDUCATION, IS THAT OF BEING A PRIORITIZED MORAL ONE?"

(*Tha* IMPORTANCE OF EDUCATION)

GOVERNMENT ACCOUNTABILITY
Held Ineffective

BU  ESS

SIN

Lies, damn lies and 'leadership Failure'. reorganization plan
A moral obligation !

"WE COULD BE IN STORE FOR SOMEWHAT OF A MILD WINTER!

Teaching THE Good Book as a Textbook

(1980) foundation of God's new world by DR. Sunday

FOUNDER OF 'THE POSITIVE FAITH RELIGION,

INFORMATION BANK: GOD is THE

UNIVERSE LENDER, OMNIPOTENT

SPENDER AND MENDER OF HEARTS

THAT ARE TENDER. PURE LOVE'S

ONE AND ONLY SENDER,

The Positive SPIRIT Without GENDER.

FOUDROYANTLY, SO MANY WOMEN TO RELIGIOUSLY EMANCIPATE,—SO LITTLE TIME.

PROPITIOUSLY AN EQUAL OPPERTUNITY EMPLOYER,

ONLY ONE UNIVERSAL GOD Bless you.

welcome to Debateland Tha big picture!

THA PURPOSE OF LIFE!

PAGE 23.

Why do some doubt that life has any purpose? WHO CAN TELL US?

A UNIQUE SOURCE of SUPERIOR WISDOM YOURS TRULY:

WITHOUT A STRUCTURED PRAYER RAPPOR TO SERVING GOD.. THEIR LEFT WITH THIS GO WITH FLOW, ROLL YOUR OWN ATTITUDE — DUDE.. AND SOME DON'T EVEN WANT TO THINK THAT THERE COULD EVER BE ANY KIND OF A RESTRICTIVE MORAL CONSCIOUSNESS.

Rules for a successful and happy life.

Score THIS a Debate Knockout ➡

Heard Any Good Sermons Lately?

Battling for Souls! where to begin:

LOS ANGELES, JUNE 1980. THIS HERE BEING THA FOUNDING STATEMENTS OF THIS NEW AGE **Religion,** WRITTEN BY DR. SUNDAY - HEAVEN ON EARTH EDUCATOR, - WITH Heaven on Earth IDEOLOGY! DOCTOR OF RELIGIOUS SCIENCE,

IN ANY MUTUALLY POSITIVE TRANSACTION.

"Tha Purpose OF Life"

is TO SERVE **GOD** ((THROUGH HUMANKIND)) ViA THA HONEST CONSIDERATE SiDE OF OUR PERSONALITIES AND DECISION MAKINGS., FOR WE'RE ALL BIRDS OF A FEATHER CREATED EMOTIONALLY EQUAL ViA CONSIDERATION, VERSUS INCONSIDERATION, POSITIVE, VERSUS NEGATIVE STIMULUS., ALL ONE IN THA SAME PEOPLE, RESPONSIBLE FOR THA SAFETY AND WELL BEING OF ALL PEOPLE.

ALL God's Children
'Apostle Lips Now'

Tha name behind Tha face

"I WANT TO LiVE IN A WORLD WHERE THERE'S A IDEOLOGICAL MESSIAH, ON EVERY CORNER."

Book store: How a Blockbuster Was Born!

When Hell Turned to Heaven How to make a point at tha speed of light, "THE NEW WORLD begins in your own backyard."

PAGE 24

teaching Kids about
GOD
is MY BEST FRIEND
AND SIDE KICK, THATS WHY I'M PSYCHIC
SOUL `SELL` DUMB
AM I LONELY...

Who am I

I'M THA GANGSTER OF LOVE, OR JUST
ANOTHER KIND OF PAGE 25, PRIEST HOOD.
I KNOW HOW TO STEAL YOUR HEART HONESTLY!

Who am I

On record

▼

I AM EURE,
AND EURE
ARE ME!

AND EURE ARE
ME, AND I
AM EURE.

now Hare This

***CREATED
"EMOTIONALLY"
EQUAL***

What's Up Doc?
JUNEAU, OLIVE IN
WE KNOW NEVADA...

credibility–

ON **How I'd Govern** ? *Turning Back tha Clock*
Not Tha Same Old Song And Dance.
`FOR I WALK SOFTLY AND CARRY A CHAPSTICK.
"**Peace On Earth** GLOBALLY SPEAKING, I PROMISE I'LL PUT
4 JIVE TURKEY, IN EVERY HOUSEHOLD."...
ALL CONTRIBUTING TO A **contagious–**philosophy

Step into my office
set tha record straight.

`2002 sex *Scandals Begin to Tarnish* CATHOLIC CHURCH NATION!, DAMAGE **has been done** . COMPOUNDING tha Shame depicts tha dark side of **hell**. "Slapping tha system IN A LOST CIVILIZATION ! I CAN DEAL WITH SAINT FRANCIS OF A SISSY, BEING THA PATRON ST. OF HOMOSEXUALS – BUT THOSE PEDOPILES NEED TO BE PROSECUTED". New Holy Road BIBLE **NEEDS** TO RID THA WORLD OF CHILD PORN... **Public-backs one** ADULT RELATIONSHIP AT A TIME AND, **or** *Priests* tha **MARRYIN' KIND.**, `OR STRICTLY BY WAY OF FREEDOM OF choice" REMAINING ABSTINENT AS USUAL. *Face Up to 'Life' according* to a new modern **DAY RELIGIOUS CLEAN SLATE.** trust can be changed ! *Ye of Any Faith,* Imagine **real world** Peace Answers to

Your guide to Tha roads less taken➡

IN REFERENCE TO THA UP AND COMING SUPER BOWL TV COMMERCIAL HOMAGE, BY STAR ATHELETE TIM TEBOW, AND COMPANY. INFORMATIVELY BAPTIZING, OR BRAIN WASHING US ALL WITH THEIR PRO-LIFE, STAND ON ABORTION! TO ALL MY GOD LOVING, RIGHTEOUS BRETHREN., OR WRITTEN BY THA 'ROCKET SCIENTOLOGIST THAT'S GONE "FATHER", OR FURTHER THEN ANY MAN. I MUST SAY THAT HISTORICALLY THA WORLD WOULD HAVE BEEN A MUCH BETTER PLACE TO LIVE HAD OSAMA BIN LADEN, BEEN 'ABORTED! ALONG WITH THA LIKES OF KHALID JJ I CAN REALLY SHAIKH 'em DOWN MOHAMMED., CHO-SEUNG-HUI-32., FORT I'M NOW A LEGITIMATE HOOL MAJ. HASAN. — YOU WANT MORE SUCKER? THIS PEN JUST BEGAN TO DANCE! HOW ABOUT LAST WEEK'S PAR FOR THA CURSE, OCTA GUN DOWN SLAUGHTERER, ETC. ETC. ETC. TOSS IN REBEL WITHOUT A BRAIN, SCOTT ROEDER! "HARANGUING, PRO-LIFE GOES INTO EFFECT THA DAY PRO-INTELLIGENCE COMES OF AGE." IN CONCLUSION: ADOLF HITLER, SHOULD HAVE BEEN ABORTED! FOR ONE — HE 'ALMOST WIPED OUT MY PARENTS DURING WWII; AND HAD EVIL SUCCEEDED, ONE WOULD HAVE NEVER GOT THA OPPORTUNITY TO READ THIS SIDE OF THA COINS INFORMATIVE RESPONSE, BY YOURS TRULY.

IN ACCORDANCE WITH THA EVOLUTION OF MASS COMMUNICATION!! MY PERSONAL BOOK THEME SONG, IS BY EMERSON, LAKE, AND PALMER, CALLED 'FROM THA BEGINNING'...

What EVERYONE ON EARTH Needs to KNOW.

Birth control is A Realistic Survival Plan.

PERSPECTIVES on Abortion controversy

" LIVING WITHIN THIS A - AFTER THA FACT SOCIETY."

Point-of-View `PRO-LIFE GOES INTO EFFECT THA DAY PRO-INTELLIGENCE, (BIRTH CONTROL) COMES OF AGE.

" CHOOSE PRO-INTELLIGENCE."

(While You Were Out MESSAGE EXTENSION) PAGE 27.

Presenting A NEW AGE BIBLICAL INTERPRETATION OF - "GO FORTH AND MULTIPLY." NOT BY WAY OF CONCEPTION - BUT BY WAY OF INTELLIGENCE. WHEREAS LET THIS BE KNOWN TO THA MASSES., TO impoverishly OVER-POPULATE A SOCIETY IS A IMPONDERABLE 'SIN !! FURTHERMORE BIRTH CONTROL CONTRACEPTION, CAN WIPE-OUT STICKER SHOCK 75%, OF THA ANNUAL ABORTIONS TAKING PLACE IN——. ON WAR: GO WHERE NO PRAYERFUL MIND HAS EVER GONE BEFORE! TO PRAY FOR PEACE ON EARTH WITHOUT BIRTH CONTROL, IS PREPOSTEROUS. THERE IS NO — SOCIAL HARMONY WITH THA OVERPOPULATING RESOURCE EXHAUSTING-GLOBAL WARMING-PHENOMENON. WORLD-WIDE, WHAT ABOUT YOUR BACK-YARD — FETUS — FEED-US — FEET-US — FEAT-US →

TODAY'S BRIEFING THA TRUTH ABOUT **Abortion**
OF Paradise & Poverty IN PERSPECTIVE:

"SHOE ON THA OTHER FOOT PROPOSAL"
FIRST IN TALK

Mr. Involvement Offers Real Solution! Ticket urges bipartisan cooperation, opens heart to family Adoption plan.

OR HOW TO TAINT ONE'S INDIVIDUAL PERCEPTION OF FEELING SO RIGHTEOUS!

"I WANT TO LIVE IN A WORLD WHERE DEEP POCKETED FAT CATS HAVE GREEN LIGHT ACCESS TO A RED HOT LINE OF PERSUASIVE ADOPTION AS OPPOSE TO ABORTION, IN THAT FINANCIALLY WHEN THA MOTHS START FLYING FROM THEIR POCKET BOOKS IN ADOPTING TEN, OR TWENTY KIDS, THEY'LL BECOME VIGIL WORKING, BILL PASSING SUPPORTERS, OF ALL MY PROPOSALS IN REFERENCE TO THIS SENSITIVE ISSUE!"

Dear Friend SETTING IT STRAIGHT ORPHANAGE CITY! THOSE GUYS THAT COMMITED VIOLENT ACTS AGAINST ABORTION CLINICS ETC, COULD HAVE GONE OUT AND WORKED 2, OR 3 JOBS DONATING ECONOMIC SUPPORT FOR THIS CAUSE, INSTEAD OF WHAT THEY DID. VATICAN CITY! Constructive criticism OK, pontiff says.

Church Unity : proposal Might add $100 billion to Support for adoptees.

CONCERNS OF This book Author SIGNED: "HEAVY DUTY INTO BIRTH CONTROL".

If Fish Could Talk...They'd "BOAT FOR ME." **life on tha beach** ⚓ ⚓

PAGE 28

QUICK READ NEWS WRAP **2001** VOTED YES, FOR Stem cell research FINANCIAL SUPPORT.

project

story in Response **Take**

I LOVE KIDS! I THINK EVERYONE WHO WINS LOTTO SHOULD GO OUT AND HAVE 10 OR 12.

WHAT BEERS?

advantage of TREATMENT FOR _____→

Who said that?

teaching kids about sexual responsibility

LETTERS TO THA EDITOR JUNE, 1986

A CRY FOR HELP BY CHANNEL TV KHJ 9 Los Angeles.

YOUR PRAYERS ANSWERED OPINION: TO WHAT WOULD BE OF GREAT HELP IN THIS EVER GROWING PROBLEM OF TEEN PREGNANCY. WHEREAS THESE INSECURE I WANT IT ALL-NOW TEENS, LACK MENTAL FORESIGHT, THUS FALLING PREY TO THIS NOW EXISTING SITUATION. THEREFORE AN ACADEMY AWARD WINNING **Movie Time** SPECIAL SYNOPSIS, WRITTEN BY YOURS TRULY, "THA PIT FALLS SUGGESTED FILMING OF "HEAVY EMPHASIS" ON THA ECONOMIC AND ENERGY DRAINING OBLIGATION IT IS TO PROPERLY BRING UP A CHILD AS A SINGLE PARENT IN THIS DAY AN AGE, RIGHT OUT OF THA ROOKERY BECOMING A REAL BIRDEN ON THEIR OWN PARENTS! THA **MOVIES** "OBJECTIVE GLAMORIZATION ON SUBJECT MATTER CAN ONLY RESULT IN MAKING MORE TEENS PREGNANT, IN THAT REALISTIC DRAMA IS THA ONLY REAL FORMAT TOWARDS THA GAINING OF ONE'S INTELLECTUAL FORESIGHT."

—————— (22 YEARS, LATER.) ——————

GLOUCESTER, Mass. ## School teens make pregnant pact

"INSECURE BABIES HAVING BABIES! IN THA GAME OF LIFE, ANY LOSER CAN GO OUT AND MAKE A BABY., ONLY A REAL WINNER CAN IN-STRIDE, APPROPRIATELY PROVIDE FOR ONE. "WAKE UP SMELL THA POVERTY." WHEREAS IN A INITIAL HOME, WHERE ONE FINDS PROPER LOVE AND GUIDANCE, (FAMILY VALUES) SELDOM DOES THIS QUAGMIRE EVER EXIST. P.S. NEXT! LIMITING YOURSELF, MOST SINGLE GUYS WON'T SETTLE DOWN WITH SOMEONE WHO HAS AN ALREADY MADE FAMILY ooo WHEREAS ANYTHING LESS OF A COMBINED COMMENTARY WOULD BE A DON'T "PHASE" ME BRO...

1985 NEWS BRIEFS Those "Good Old Days"

Writer traces roots of religion

DR. SUNDAY **Story** VS. DARWIN

A MONOTHEISTICAL POINT OF VIEW!

"FOR GOD, CREATED THA UP AND ADAM APE STRUCTRED MAN, THAT WE EVE-VOLVED **controversy**." **Publishing**

"**Reality Remains.** FEELINGS OF BEING GIVEN THA TOWER OF BABEL ROUTINE, OR WHAT PART OF DEMOCRACY DON'T THEY UNDERSTAND? I'M THA SOMEBODY THAT NOBODY CAN ACCEPT, FOR I'M THA NOBODY THAT WILL SOMEDAY BE ACCEPTED."

POINT OF VIEW It's all inline:

This Classroom Connection is brought to you By Tha Founder of THE POSITIVE Faith Religion.

(Notes From All Over) Take This Exam!

"HOW TO SAY SOMETHING IN SO MANY WORDS." HE WAS THA ORIGINAL-APOSTLES. RECOMMENDED, ON HOW TO OVER-THROW AN OPPRESSIVE GOVERNMENT BY WAY OF PROCLAIMING HIMSELF TO BE GOD, EXPERIMENT."

OR NAME THA JOYOUS EVENTS THAT TOOK PLACE RIGHT AFTER HE, OR ANY-MAN THAT EVER PROCLAIMED TO BE GOD, HAPPENED?

Show and Tell

Secrets From Tha History of an Old Idea

Tha Making of 'HIStory'

Class 101: Global Mythmaking

written 1983

THA GOVERNMENT AND it's MEDIA BELIEVES THAT JESUS CHRIST IS GOD, AS MUCH AS A HERION ADDICT BELIEVES IN SANTA CLAUS!

But

AS LONG AS THEY CAN KEEP YOU SWEET-N-LOW THAT SOME MAN IS OR WAS FAR MORE HONORABLE THAN YOURSELF: TO ALL OPPRESSED PEOPLE! A PENNY FOR YOUR THOUGHTS.

personal RESPONSIBILITY?

WHAT GOOD IS IT TO HAVE A RELIGION WHERE YOU'VE GOT ONE INIMITABLE SUPER HERO, AND FOR THA MOST PART THA REST OF US ARE ALL BEING LOOKED UPON AS UNJUSTIFIABLE MONKEYS UNCLES., IN THAT TOSS IN A GUILT FREE TRIP - "HE DIED FOR OUR SINS - SO LET'S GO FOR THA GUSTO."

is **JESUS CHRIST** your personal savior of nation's

VIA a **Scam**? **examine** Book reviews **Incredible evidence.** Here's why A COMMITMENT TO truth:

Bullfighters, you've reached this page 32, Be a "lookie Lou"

once upon a time *Rising star* wins fiction prize!

J.C **Cult Man** versus government *in a*

Fragile society: APOSTLE *Recommended* MEDIA PLANNER;

religious honoree Simple Solution **he might be able to** with a G—OD,

coming-out party **reform** Hype Alert **politicians.** Dream On

"We are one, we are human!"

IMAGINE IF THERE WAS A YOURS TRULY RELIGION, THAT COULD FREE US FROM ALL THA INSANITY - AND WE COULD LIVE LIFE AS ONE...SIGNED: "HOORAY FOR OUR SIDE."

This New Age religion analyst, puts you in touch.
Statement of Faith! AMERICA, AMERICA, GOD SHED HIS
`THY GRACE ON ME. Project Restart

Follow-up On PAGE 40

Facing Up to Reality

THE ONE and only GOD

PERFORMS MIRACLES.
NOT STRUCTURED MAN.
BUT THROUGH MAN BY GOD.
NOW THATS THE POSITIVE SPIRIT.

New Age religion REVIEW & OUTLOOK

FINAL INSULT AS Jesus Christ, HIT MARY MAGDALENE, WITH A STONE FACE AND RESPONDED —

HONEY, I SHRUNK 'THE KIDS.'

ALL God's Children PAGE 33

Tha Last Days of a Dynasty.

For a lot of Captives it's a dead end!

GOSPEL FICTIONS

"_Turning 'Wine into Water'._"

THA LAST SUPPER. 'WHEN JESUS INFORMED THA APOSTLES THAT HE, WASN'T GOING TO BE AROUND FOR THA NEXT KNIGHTS OF COLUMBUS SHINDIG — THEY ALL STARTED GUZZLING DOWN THEIR WINE AS IF IT WERE WATER.

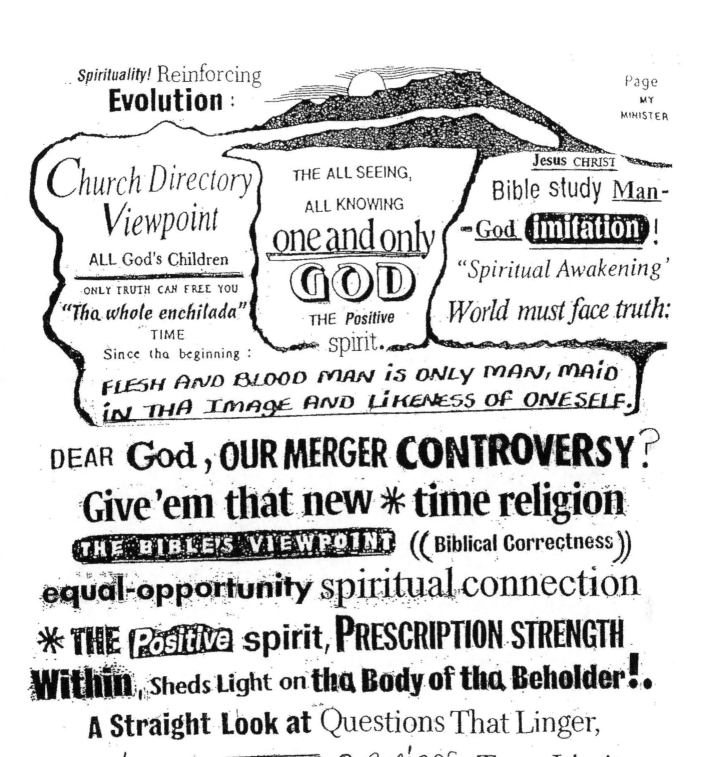

*C*hurch Directory
Viewpoint

ALL God's Children

ONLY TRUTH CAN FREE YOU

"Tha whole enchilada"
TIME
Since tha beginning :

THE ALL SEEING,
ALL KNOWING
one and only
G⊙D
THE Positive
spirit.

Jesus CHRIST
Bible study **Man-**
-**God** imitation !
"Spiritual Awakening'
World must face truth:

FLESH AND BLOOD MAN IS ONLY MAN, MAID
IN THA IMAGE AND LIKENESS OF ONESELF.

DEAR **God , OUR MERGER CONTROVERSY**?

Give'em that new * time religion

THE BIBLE'S VIEWPOINT ((Biblical Correctness))

equal-opportunity spiritual connection

* THE Positive spirit, PRESCRIPTION STRENGTH

Within, Sheds Light on tha Body of tha Beholder !..

A Straight Look at Questions That Linger,

DECODING THA TRINITY 3 AMIGOS Term Limits.

Say It Ain't So, enjoy your retirement page 34.

'Mighty Mary's prayer benefit falls pray

to A NEW Disneyland adventure • Reality Check

Tha Party's Over •

IN A Humane Society
you Do tha right thing,

IS tha American Way!

"MOSQUE MADNESS PREMONITION." AUGUST, 2010
'IN THA NEWS'

IN REFERENCE TO THA 'WE KNOW WHAT'S GOOD FOR YOU, TAX PAYER SPONSORED - KORAN IT DOWN THEIR THROATS, GROUND ZERO MOSQUE — THAT 77% OPPOSE! INSENSITIVITY? TO HAVE, NO RIGHTEOUS CONSIDERATION FOR THA MAJORITY OF OTHER PEOPLES FEELINGS IS EQUIVALENT TO THA PROMOTION OF A ROLL YOUR OWN, PHARISAICAL RELIGIOUS ALLAH CARTE. PAR FOR THA CURSE PREDICTION.. BECAUSE NO U.S. CONSTRUCTION FIRM WILL BUILD IT. THEY'LL PROBABLY GREEN CARD IN, CONSTRUCTION CREWS FROM YEMEN AND SOMALIA, ALL WITH DEMOLITION BACKGROUNDS. BUILD BY DAY = BLOW-UP OTHER PARTS OF THA CITY BY NIGHT! THUS THANKING ALLAH, FOR INFIDEL CLEANSING LONG WEEKENDS., AND FINALLY, FLAT OUT IN THA MIDST OF WINTER IN A CENTRAL PARK SETTING, SOME FLIRTATIOUS BOLD PUNDIT WILL BE ASKING DAISY KHAN.. (CON) DO YOU SUPPORT SHARIA LAW? — AND HER RESPONSE WILL BE, OF COURSE I DO! WHEREAS IN A MATRICULATING HEART BEAT, ALL THA LOCALS WILL RESPOND BY PELTING HER WITH SNOWBALLS ...

'PAGE = MY
I—MUMMY'

♫ Give'em some of that new-time religion ♫
"... And They Lived Happily Ever After."

written OPINION COMMENTARY | FROM THE ORIGINAL GHOSTWRITER RESEARCH FOUNDATION

quotes Observations, confessions and revelations

New Age **Make a difference** Bible School

CHALLENGING FALSE IMAGES OF WORSHIP Page 34 1/4
THUS WORTHY OF BECOMING A NOBEL PPIZE WINNER...

BIBLE-BELT CHURCH DESTROYING TORNADOES, ETC. FLOODS, DROUGHTS, EARTHQUAKES, HURRICANES-BLAME IT ON THA RIO FALSE GOD, 'SONWORLD EXHIBIT!
LIKEWISE, HOW ABOUT THA EASTER ISLAND 'FALSE GOD, STATUE WORSHIP STORY, OF ALL THOSE PEOPLE THAT VANISHED. 'YOU CAN'T TOSS THE BOSS FOR A LOSS! TO CASTAWAY FROM ONE'S ALLEGIANCE TO GOD, OR ROLL YOUR OWN LIFE-STYLE, IS TO OPEN THA FLOOD GATES TO A ATMOSPHERIC NEGATIVE SPIRITED, THYCON SITTING MONSTROSITY! (HISTORY 1927, REVISITED ETC. EXAMPLES)
START OF WORK ON THA -DON'T TRY TO CON-GOD, THE POSITIVE SPIRIT., ABOUT YOUR FALSE GOD CREATION, OR CELEBRATION OF MT. RUSHMORE, THUS 'GOLDEN FLEECE, IN THAT SAY CHEESE, GOD ONLY PICTURED US HERE! RESULTING IN THA 1929, STOCK MARKET CRASH., ALONG WITH THA 30'S DUST BOWL, AND DEPRESSION., LEADING ALL THA WAY UP TO THA 1941, COMPLETION OF MT. RUSHMORE, AND THA WELCOMING INTO WW II, OR 'HELL ON EARTH PERSONIFIED."

INSTANTANEOUS TRANSFORMATION ?

CURE FOR THA COMMON CURSE! 'NEVER IN ANY SITUATION SAY YOU HAVE FAITH IN SOME PERSON; WHEREAS TO SAY YOU HAVE CONFIDENCE WILL DO...

"LAYING THA GROUND WORK FOR A BIG TIME RELIGIOUS/POLITICO TERM OF OFFICE. THA WORDS, SEPARATION OF CHURCH AND STATE, ARE 'NOT FOUND IN THA CONSTITUTION."

GOSPEL FICTIONS
REFORM TAKES SHAPE
A Straight Look at Questions That Linger,

NO EXPIRATION DATE

CHURCH

EXPRESSES FEAR of

PAGE **34½**

Car 54 / Car 54

GOD

OR GOD-FEARING PEOPLE. **Beyond tha Scare** replaced by
New gospel THEORY POSITIVE RAIN, NEGATIVE RAIN!

IF YOU SHOULD ASK ME! HOW CAN THERE BE ANY
FEAR of GOD, WHEN IN FACT ALL THA GOOD MOR-
PHOLOGICAL ELEMENTS OF ENJOYABLE LIFE AND
HUMANISTIC RELATIONSHIPS, CAN ONLY BE ATTRI-
BUTED TO THE ALWAYS WAS, AND ALWAYS WILL
BE, ATMOSPIRIT WORKING POSITIVE. THE

POSITIVE Spirit COMETH Teaching of New Age TRUTHS
DOCTOR'S BOOK OF NEW World REMEDIES
A UNIQUE SOURCE of SUPERIOR WISDOM

Tha Dead Restored to Life
15 "There is going to be a resurrection of both THA righteous and THA unrighteous." —Acts 24:15.

16 "Tha hour is coming in which all those in tha memorial tombs [God's memory] will hear God's voice and come out."—John 5: 28, 29.

FOLLOW-UP ON PAGE 64.

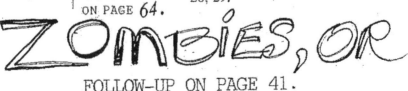

ZOMBIES, OR

FOLLOW-UP ON PAGE 41.

5 MINUTES TO FREEDOM

TODAY "**i** **MUST** **CONfESS**

Book Logline

A Logline is a short, very short brief description of what your book is about. Try to make the description as exciting and enticing as possible, you want to really hook potential readers to purchase your book.

I.Q. YOU iiN ON this **Smart** & **Final** Testimony!

"Losing THEiR RELiGiON AND GAiNiNG MiNE, OR MERGERS FiNENESS HOUR? SIGNED BY YOURS TRULY, ANTi- CHRiST SUPERSTAR"...

♪ (((WHO ARE YOU?))) ♪

MEET THE NEW BOSS, NOT THE SAME AS THE OLD BOSS! .

spiritual connection

"♪ EVERYTHiNG'S MADE TO BE BROKEN, I JUST WANT YOU, TO KNOW WHO I AM ♪"

SiGNED: EMANCiPATOR EXTRAORDiNAR

"**Let freedom truly reign**"

Vintage Journalism *Don't Touch That Dial*

HIS TIME IS
NOW

DISCOUNT BABY

Today's focus Public Entity

666

Everybody's had their shot at him

Front Page News

Now it's his turn.

Founder of The POSITIVE Faith Religion.

Tha Fight for Tha Right to Preach.

When a man lives to help others

IT'S NO SECRET

EVIL NEEDS TO BE AFRAID

 page and you

PAGE 36. miss a lot →

"Spiritual Awakening"

Whaddya gonna do America?

HIS DAY IN COURT = summon.,

deliveries faster than pizza

join protest STACK PAGES HAVE IT ALL !

"'This Is My Life' Years haven't been kind.
words surely can change meanings,
666 gave his name to a county.

Why settle for a cheap imitation

THA SEARCH FOR SIGNS OF INTELLIGENT LIFE IN THA UNIVERSE?

OZborn no different then tha man behind tha shroud, OR tha curtain.,

INTHAT I WAS BORN OF A VIRGIN, FOR MY MOTHER WAS ONCE A VIRGIN...

INTRODUCING *THA WARM AND FUZZY SIDE OF BEING 666'.*

(WALK IN MY SHOES COPYRIGHTED.)

LEADER OF THA MUZZLE'em FAITH SOCIETY..

————— EVERYBODY KNEW I'D BE A MUZZLE'em. —————

"**Book facts**— SHOW STOPPER = ASBESTOS AS I KNOW. " JAQUIN ON WATER "

— OVER AN ILLUSIONARY ICE POND OR PUDDLE. ((VERSUS)) THA OVER-ALL
IMPORTANCE OF JAQUIN ALL-OVER BUREAUCRATIC GRID-LOCK;
THAT'S SOMETHING HE COULD NEVER DO;
AS WE WITNESSED IN HIS INTERVIEW WITH BARBARA WALTERS,
SOME 2,000 YEARS AGO...

journalists answers to a brave new world

Letters to Tha editor, 1993 — RENO GAZETTE-JOURNAL

(QUOTABLE QUOTES, FROM A YOURS TRULY, ENDING ESSAY.)

I NEVER MET A ""NICE"" MAN, I DIDN'T LIKE.

Cloud Nine THE VIEW FROM TOP

HISTORICALLY—WITH ALL THA FOREIGN LANGUAGE NAME PRONUNCIATIONS
FOR GOD! —GAZING DOWNWARD UPON ONE'S VERBAL PRAYER REQUEST,.
'GOD WAS FIRST TO MAKE THE STATEMENT!

You Talkin' To Me?

AUTHOR'S NOTE: CHALK ONE UP FOR ALL ENGLISH SPEAKING!
(COMMON DENOMINATOR) WE ALL LAUGH AND CRY IN THA SAME LANGUAGE.
GLOBALLY SPEAKING, NOW ALL WE HAVE TO DO IS FILL IN THA GAPS...

Closing arguments take center stage

Bible study Legacy *Jesus Christ*

super star missing in action

NO STRINGS ATTACHED
Running on dead batteries faces shareholders PAGE 38 'battle

of his life? FINAL DAYS ! **In Search of a Sequel** ?

A Sondance EXTRA-LIFE return **Guide to** SAVE *tha* WORLD

Skywalk **INSURANCE** Conspiracy Period **Over...**

What's Next ? OPERATION Hidden World Discovery of **a**

Simply Smarter Minimum Wager , **OR HELL!** WHAT'S A NICE

guy LIKE me DOING iN A PLACE LIKE THIS?

Pieces Beginning to Fall

Into ~"HALO EVERYBODY OUR TIME STARTS AT
— NOW YOU KNOW **Atrocities :**

Be sure to teach them about →

Powerful Testimony: PUBLIC — FOR — UM

"LAYING THA GROUND WORK FOR A BIG TIME RELIGIOUS/POLITICO TERM OF OFFICE. THA WORDS = SEPARATION OF CHURCH AND STATE, ARE 'NOT FOUND IN THA CONSTITUTION."

seeing our way clear

♫ TO MANY CHURCHS, AND NOT ENOUGH TRUTH! 🎼

" The Gospel according to If you Build This."

=== 15, CENTURIES OF UP IN COMING FAME ???

🎼 IT'S THA END OF THA WORLD AS WE KNOW IT. ♪♪ **no?**

Then "FINAL DAZE" is A 'WELCOME TO HELL', MAKE SURE THEY ISSUE YOU A PITCH FORK!

This Week's Biggest Releases

IN REGARDS TO THA ANTICIPATION OF A GLORIFIED CELESTIAL BEING ???

"YOU CAN FOOL SOME OF THA PEOPLE SOME OF THA TIME. AND MOST OF THA PEOPLE MOST OF THA TIME. , ETC---

FEELING TOTALLY PRESSURED JESUS, POPS RIGHT OUT OF THA 'CLODS LIKE SOME KIND OF A SYFY DIVINE, INIMITABLE PERFECTIONIST, WITH A ILLUMINATING COLLECTION PLATE. REALISTIC COMPATIBILITS?

Oops! your WAKE up CALL.

Objectivity SANITIES FINEST HOUR! **Biblical Correctness,**

This Classroom Connection quotes (AUTHOR'S PERSONAL POINT OF VIEW)

"FOR I AM 'NO BETTER THEN ANY HUMAN-KIND PERSON, IN ANY HUMAN-KIND SITUATION." SPEAKS VOLUMES...

Reassuring POWER TO THE PEOPLE,.

Political football: Half Time at tha Revolution PAGE 39.

Vote, YES *on* Praiseworthy:

RENO GAZETTE-JOURNAL *PRINTED YOURS TRULY BACK IN* JULY 1992.

LETTERS TO THA EDITOR.

Question SHOULD PRAYER BE ALLOWED AT PUBLIC SCHOOL FUNCTIONS?

Armed With tha Constitution YES. *TAKEN IN PROPER CONTEXT TO USE THA WORD NAME GOD, AND 'ONLY THA WORD NAME GOD, WITHOUT COERCION OF AND SPECIFIC RELIGION.'* IS LEAVING A INDIVIDUAL WITH ONE'S

OWN PERSONAL CONCEPT THAT CAN BE VERY ENLIGHTENING FOR THIS DAY AND AGE.

"*WITHOUT COERCION CONCEPTS OF GOD WORKS FOR ALL*"...

A Common Denominator - (EXAMPLE) IN GOD WE TRUST. PAGE 40

"MY THOUGHTS EXACTLY; OR CLOSE ENOUGH FOR RELIGIOUS WORK."

This Classroom Connection is brought to you By

RELIGIOUSLY SPEAKING, OR WRITTEN BY THA
ROCKET-SCIENTOLOGIST THATS GONE "FATHER"
OR FURTHER THEN ANY MAN. ((CHA--CHING))

"ALWAYS REMEMBER, EVERYTIME A CASH REGISTER BELL RINGS

FROM THA PURCHASE OF THIS BOOK, AN ANGEL GET'S THEIR WINGS."

WELCOME TO SUNDAY SCHOOL,

Bible **Deciphering** reform plan

Time to 'Rescue tha Flintstone Judeo-Christian *Once Upon A Time* Bible'.

1989. **quote** John Shelby Spong. Episcopal bishop of Newark, New Jersey.

RE-EDITED *MUCH* "improved" version of *Written* BY YOURS TRULY,

THA LITTERAL INTERPETATIONS OF THA BIBLE HAVE FOSTERED SOME OF THA MOST HIDEOUS OF INSTITUTIONS SUCH AS WAR AND REVENGE," MANY A CASE OF SOLE SEARCHING DELUSIONAL PSYCOTIC CRIME, SUCH AS JIM JONES, OR DAVID KORESH, ETC." INFERIOR FUROR, OR THA HITLER BIBLE READING COURSE OF "CHOSEN PEOPLE" ANTI-SEMITISM. THA SUBJUGATION OF WOMEN. HOMOPHOBIA. CONDONATION OF SLAVERY VIA ECONOMIC OPPRESSION.

"A BOOK RESPONSIBLE FOR THESE STATEMENTS THUS INACTMENTS, CANNOT BE IN ANY LITERAL SENSE THE TRUE WORD OF God. ⟶

"THE WORLD TOMORROW."
"All God's children".
Tha BATTLE TO SAVE OUR PLANET

TULIPS ARE BETTER THAN ONE, OR READ MY TULIPS !

*"IN THAT THA BIBLE IS ALL IN ALL MORE ANCIENT
HUMAN STANDARD CREATED THEN GOD INSPIRED.
CONSPICUOUSLY THA BIBLE IS A BOOK OF SYMBOLIC RATHER
THEN LITERAL VERSES, OR UNSCIENTIFIC ILLOGICAL HUMAN
FABLES THRU OLD-TIME MORAL PRECEPTS. THEREFORE IN
NEED OF LIBERATION FROM ITS OWN TEACHINGS, TO BE
UPDATED AND REWRITTEN FOR THA PEOPLE OF OUR TIMES,
AND ALL TIMES"..*

A work of monumental religious and political significance.

(WRITTEN IN 1983, BY YOURS TRULY.)

PORTRAITS OF EXTRAORDINARY LIVES

Celebrating Years of New Stories About Our Most Outstanding People and Events.

What's New ? "Real World" *breakthrough* ! THE BIBLE
of a new age **GREATEST BOOK EVER WRITTEN** *Recounting*
'restructuring' **Rewriting Life Stories** *and Reviewing*
WORLD history. *Teaming Up for New Discoveries* !
FORMULA to Prophecy **declared dead awaken to A new life .**
News youth can use: IMAGINE YOURSELF IN

THE Living BIBLE, *Angels put in right field*
WILL BE UP DATED AND ETERNALLY OPEN.
PAYING HOMAGE TO ALL INSPIRATIONAL
AND INGENIOUS PROPHETS.*, can all but guarantee

your spot on bestseller list. ANNOUNCING AUTHENTIC Bible Prophecy !

YOU CAN BUY **in** . *Worldwide Recognition* , history made available to you.

MAGIC KINGDOM CLUB Spotlight *on* EXTRA BUNDLES !

PASSING OF TIME 'SINS' WILL SOON BE FORGIVEN.

Teaching 'THE Good Book as a
ACADEMY AWARDS
programing
TESTIMONY TO GOOD LIVING IN
A PERFORMANCE ARTIST!

WRITTEN BY A FORMER EMPLOYEE
OF THA MONTH AT DIAL A PRAYER./
LOSING THEIR RELIGION AND GAINING
"HOW I got Religion ACTORS."
This *Doesn't Take A Genius* To figure out
Tha Rise of a Star Reformer.

ENROLLMENT

COMMON KNOWLEDGE IS TO KNOW GOD LOVES
YOU, AND THAT GOD IS FORGIVING., IN THAT
TO CLAIM THA REALITY OF MORAL RELIGIOUS
CONVICTION, IS IN ALWAYS BEING WORTHY OF
GOD'S LOVE. ACTIVATING **SCRIPT.** LIGATURE.

Lights, Camera, *Soul Mission* **Born-Again ...**

Tha Art of Restoring Magnetic Heads

"Presenting GOD'S INSPIRED WORD".

♩♩ MA-MA, DON'T LET YOUR BABIES GROW-UP TO BE COW'ARDS. ♩♩

"BULLY PREVENTION CLINIC"
"You can quote me"

AS THIS MAVERICK 'PREACHER WILL TELL YOU.

CAN ' YOU SAY THAT IT TAKES ONE OF TREMENDOUS

MORAL STRENGTH TO DO GOOD, OR RIGHT ?

Train Like a Pro,
" i can."

THIS HERE STORY IS ABOUT THIS 'PRIORITIZED MORALLY

SAMSONIAN MAN, AND HIS GOD,

TAKING ON ALL OF AL-QAIDA!

((THA' POSITIVE RESULTS ARE IN))

"THEY HAVEN'T GOT A PRAYER".

equal-opportunity spiritual connection?

(((Biblical Correctness)))

IM PRUV ALL Seminar

THE Positive spirit, **PRESCRIPTION STRENGTH**

Within, Sheds Light on **tha Body of tha Beholder**!.

DOCTOR'S BOOK OF NEW World **REMEDIES**

programing

personal **RESPONSIBILITY** ...

Religious Science training program

SOME OF THA BRIGHTEST LEGAL MINDS
NEVER WENT TO LAW SCHOOL.

←— IN REFERENCE TO HATE CRIMES —→

Rewriting Life Stories We Are All Connected

FAMILY VALUES / NEW AGE PRAYER OF PRAYERS

THIS IS my **BRAIN ON** REPEAT DIALING, OR HOW TO EXPLAIN FOR ROCKET SCIENCE, BECAUSE THIS ONE'S GOING TO TAKE US ALL THA WAY TO ECUMENICAL HEAVEN! — TO LIVE IN A FREE SPEACH WORLD WHERE THERE'S AN INTELLI-GENT PERSON BORN EVERY MINUTE, IN THAT TO FIND POSITIVE SAMENESS WITHIN YOUR FELLOW MAN, IS TO FIND PEACE ON EARTH SANENESS... SETTING THA QUALITY STANDARD...

2005 ECUMENICAL heaven? RE-WRITING HISTORY.. MAYBE THA POPE'S LAST SPOKEN WORDS SHOULD HAVE BEEN QUOTED AS SAYING! "IF YOU BEHAVE YOURSELVES, YOU'LL ALL GET TO SEE ME LATER."

Based on logic." **THE POSITIVE** Faith **Religion** SIDER THESE FACTS:
"BIRTH IS TERMINAL — AND YOU ONLY GO AROUND ONCE."
"WE'RE ALL VISITORS OF THIS PLANET, PLAN IT. L.M.T. 1980 "
"WE ALL LIVE TO BE SOMEBODYS MEMORIES."
"WE'RE ALL SNOWMEN UNDER SUN LAMPS."

REVIEW & OUTLOOK

"Storytelling new way of life Example."
3 U.S. citizens killed in Yemen. Dec, 30th 2002

HERE WE GO AGAIN WITH THAT SAME OLD EXCUSE BY A DEFENDANT! ANOTHER/"G—OD TOLD ME, TO KILL THOSE PEOPLE, STORY."

Own A Moment In Time

BASED ON A ANCIENT BIBLICAL, BELIEF SYSTEM THAT G—OD TOLD ABRAHAM, TO TAKE THA LIFE OF ABE'S SON IN A RITUAL SACRIFICE. THEN RENEGED! READING BETWEEN THA LINES IN REALITY IS AN UNEXPLAINED DUEL SPIRITUAL CONFRONTATION THAT WENT ON. ✳ GOD, THE POSITIVE SPIRIT, THE HOLY SPIRIT, WOULD NEVER MINDFULLY SUGGEST TO ANYONE, THIS KIND OF NEGATIVE DELUSIONAL BEHAVIOR, IN THA FIRST PLACE. IN RETROSPECT THIS WEAK-MINDED DEFENDANT WAS DANCING TO THA INVASION OF A NEGATIVE SUGGESTIVE THOUGHT CONCEPT., OR IF YOU WILL! **godzilla** THA BEAST IN **man.** SUGGESTED FOLLOW-UP STORY *in CRIME & PUNISHMENT* CHAPTER.

CHART YOUR COURSE TO a Better
improvement OF INTERNATIONAL history

(((HISTORY REPEATS ITSELF)))

"DUBYA, ON FAITH BASED INITIATIVE,. WE WELCOME **All** FAITHS IN AMERICA." YEAH, RIGHT **!** / CONTESTABLY SPEAKING, FOR GOODNESS <u>SNAKE</u>. <u>ADAM</u> & <u>EVE</u>, WEREN'T THA FIRST TWO PEOPLE ON EARTH., MOST LIKELY THEY WERE THA FIRST TWO LITERATE PEOPLE THAT HAD THA CHANCE TO PASS ALONG THEIR STORIES! AS THA STORY GOES — <u>EDEN</u> AT HIS HEART, SOCIABLY <u>ADAM</u> <u>RIBBED</u> EVE INTO SPENDING THA WEEKEND AT A LOCAL NUDIST CAMP. ONCE THEY GOT IN THERE SHE REALIZED SHE, WAS THA <u>APPLE</u> OF HIS EYE. <u>EVE</u> THEN TRIED TO ENTICE HIM INTO TAKING <u>AN ILLEGAL</u> <u>SUBSTANCE</u>! TOTALLY FREAKED, HE RAN OVER AND PUT ON HIS CAMP <u>FORBIDDEN</u> <u>FRUIT</u> OF THA LOOM SKIVVIES, AND *THEY* BOTH GOT **86.** *PARADISE* ...

CAPITALIZE ON His positive imagination
Big Time Christian Church controversy.

"DECODING THA PARALLELS"

INTRODUCING THA PREDESTINATE, PREDICATORY, PERSPICACIOUS, PROGNOSTICATOR:
'OR NEW KID ON THA BLOCK, ((ANTI-J.C.)) (VERSUS) J.C.‽

BORN IN THA VICINITY OF BETHLEHEM STEEL OR FACTORY AIR, (VERSUS) FACTORY HEIR! RAISED IN SIN --- CITY, OR HISTORIC CALUMET CITY. 5 LETTERS FIRST NAME, 6 LETTERS LAST. I WAS BORN OF A VIRGIN FOR MY MOTHER WAS ONCE A VIRGIN; WAS THA LION WHO DID AN 8 YEAR STINT, IN A PAROCHIAL SCHOOL AS A NON-BELIEVER CAT-LICK; WHO'S CHALLENGING THIS ORIGINAL CATHOLIC. ((ANTI-J.C. ONCE WAS A SCHOOL BUS DRIVER AND A PLAYGROUND SUPERVISOR, WHO TAUGHT TRUTHS TO THA CHILDREN OF NAPERVILLE; WAS WORKING AS A CARPENTERS HELPER WHEN I OPENED MY FIRST SAVINGS ACCOUNT. HE DIED AT 33, I STARTED WRITING AT 33. A PHILOSOPHICAL 'TOTAL OPPOSITE TO HITLER, ALONG WITH 'TOTAL OPPOSITE BIRTH DATES BEING APRIL 20th (VERSUS) OCTOBER 20th; INTHAT YOURS TRULY, COMPATIBLE TO "ALL" A LIBRA SCALE BRAIN LEFTY.

== I'M THA SOMEBODY THAT NOBODY CAN ACCEPT, FOR I'M THA NOBODY THAT WILL SOMEDAY BE ACCEPTED! THA COACH OF THA HORSES, OR THA WORK HORSE THAT ISN'T A PHONY. THA LINK THAT'S GOING TO LINE YOU, AND THA LINE THAT'S GOING TO LINK YOU. ELOQUENTLY BEING THA STAGE WITHIN YOUR WORLD THAT HAS A GOOD PART FOR EVERYBODY. THA IMAGINATION WE'RE ALL PRODUCTS OF, OR THA POSITIVE IMAGINATION; PROPHETICALLY THA SEEDED WONDER, THAT SUPERSEDES THA SEEDLESS WONDER; FOR THEN MAY WE ALL BE SEATED. THA PROPHET THAT BELIEVES IN PROFIT SHARING. THA SHRINK THAT HAS NO INTENTIONS OF SHRINKING ANYONE, OR THA PILL YOU CAN ALL TAKE. WHEREFORE I'M THA MONK AMONG YOU, THAT WILL NEVER STOP MONKEYING AROUND. PERTINACIOUSLY THA SNAKE CHARMER YOU DON'T HAVE TO GRASP FOR. THA ROCKNE, YOU DON'T HAVE TO KNEE TO; A AMOS ALONZO STAG, PROTEGE TYPE ALL-AMERICAN. THA LIP TONGUE SENT FROM KRIPTON - WITH TRUTH, JUSTICE, AND 'THE POSITIVE WAY.

= FOR ALL THOSE PARALLELS ARE TRUE, EXCEPT I'M 'NOT THAT SAME JEW; I'M JUST THA BUD THAT'S WISER.

"I WANT TO LIVE IN A WORLD WHERE THERE'S MORE BUGLERS THEN BURGLARS; WHEREAS EVERY COWARD HAS A SILVER LINING. APPROPRIATELY MORE HARLEQUINS THEN HOOLIGANS. I MAY ONLY HAVE A COUPLE OF SKELETONS IN MY CLOSET, BUT ATLEAST I DON'T HAVE ANY DINOSAUR BONES. I WANT TO LIVE IN A WORLD WHERE THA IRON CLAD FOOT OF OPPRESSION BECOMES A HUSHPUPPY. U.S. ARMY DRAFTED AND QUALIFIED AS A MARKSMAN BUT, THA SOLDIER THAT WAS HANDED THA SHARPSHOOTERS MEDAL, BECAUSE THEY RAN OUT OF MARKS MEN. ..NEWS MEDIA SIGNED, AND READY FOR THA ALL S-T-A-R-E GAME...

THA KING'S SPEECH- 'Life according to a new modern

DAY RELIGIOUS CLEAN SLATE.

World must face truth: IN ALL OF LIFES GAMES
THE POSITIVE SPIRIT *
HISTORY HAS PROVEN THAT ANY 'STRUCTURED
MAN' CAN BE REPLACED. (EXAMPLES IN TIME)
FOOTBALL, WALTER PAYTON. SWIMMING, MARK SPITZ.
BASEBALL BABE RUTH, religion Jesus Christ.
"FOR ONLY **GOD,** AND THESE HERE RELIGIOUS
BOOK TRUTHS, CAN NEVER BE REPLACED."
BY WAY of THA KING DAVID, STICKS & STONES
PHILOSOPHY; OR 'AFFECTIONATELY SPEAKING!
" I CONSIDER MYSELF PROUD TO BE."

In tune with **labels** A MULTICULTORAL **White** HISPANIC,
or ACCORDING TO THA HISTORIANS WHO SAY THAT WE
ALL ORIGINATED FROM AFRICA ? AN AFRICAN-AMERICAN !
NOTHING MORE NOR NOTHING LESS THAN A
FIVE FOOT EIGHT INCH, SPANISH BLUE EYED
IRISH, LIMEY PART JEW, AND PART TOMMY
HAWK TACOBENDER TOO. A HISTORIC DEC. PARALLEL BIRTH-
DATE OR **A SEVEN MONTH PREMATURE BABY** BORN 10/20/46.
GOVERNMENTAL HISTORY BATING AND OR THA
CHALLENGING of GOD'S WILL, THERE ONCE
WAS A TIME IN MY DAY, THAT A FULL-BLOODED
JEW COULDN'T RUN FOR PRESIDENT! THEREFORE
ENTER YOURS TRULY, AND BECOME A WITNESS TO
NEWS OF RECORD on THA CREATION OF PAGE 44½

LIFE IN THESE UNITED STATES:
eating news and notes

ATLEAST ONCE A MONTH IN ANTICIPATION OF GLOBAL HARMONY, IN THIS MAN'S RELIGION INSTEAD OF MATAZH, WE EAT PIZZA. DOGMA ACCORDING TO THIS MAN'S RELIGION = ON EVERY 2ND TUESDAY OF EVERY MONTH YOU'RE NOT ALLOWED TO EAT FISH-HEAD TACOS:, ALONG WITH ON EVERY 3RD THURSDAY OF EVERY MONTH, YOU'RE NOT ALLOWED TO EAT ANY PORK RIND SNACK MUNCHIES, INTHAT SHOULD YOU FIND YOURSELF INDULGING ON THOSE DAYS, YOUR PENANCE WILL BE THAT OF "SAYING FREE OUR FATHERS AND 'THROW TWO HAIL MARY'S." (ALL IN SOLIDARITY OF THIS AUTHOR'S EXCRUCIATING CONQUEST.)

LATITUDINARIAN COMMUNION ANYONE? POLITICIANS LOVE TO HAVE NEANDERTHAL RELIGION SHOVED DOWN THA THROATS OF COMMON FOLK PEOPLE IN HOPES THAT THEY'LL ALL BEHAVE THEMSELVES; IN THAT COMMON FOLK PEOPLE WOULD LOVE TO HAVE NEANDERTHAL RELIGION SHOVED DOWN THA THROATS OF POLITICIANS IN HOPES OF OBTAINING BETTER POLICIES...

How I'd Govern! A Closer Look at

THA PUBLIC SERPENT, OR CHARMING SNAKE, THAT WOULD TAKE THA BITE OUT OF SHADY POLITICS AND SERUM IN THA RIGHT DIRECTION. INCISIVELY, EVERYONE HAS A POTENTIAL GOOD BOOK IN THEM, IF THEY COULD ONLY FIND A GOOD INTERPRETER. **'I Will Speak Out'** PAGE 45.

TIME CAPSULE—What ever happened to spoken 'for tha good of tha country'?

Sell More of What You Write !

positive vision for our future ?

on Court ruling How I'd *judge this,*

(1987)

INNERSOUL SUPPORT SYSTEM ! GOD AMONG MEN

Live, From Heaven ."Affirmative Action:

Renewing America

GOD
(WORKING THROUGH MAN)

WHEREVER ONE (FINDS) SOCIOECONOMIC
JUSTIFICATION THROUGH PRIVATE OR
GOVERNMENTAL LEGISLATION, ONE
(FINDS) THE POSITIVE SPIRIT OF GOD.
WHEREVER ONE (GIVES) SOCIOECONOMIC
JUSTIFICATION THROUGH PRIVATE OR
GOVERNMENTAL LEGISLATION, ONE HAS
WITHIN ONESELF, THE POSITIVE SPIRIT OF GOD.
(That should be some indication.)

Creating New Frontiers:

Just when you thought you'd seen everything. ▶

How to Interpret That Heavenly Knowledge

𝔚𝔥𝔞𝔱 𝔖𝔞𝔦𝔱𝔥 𝔗𝔥𝔢 𝔖𝔠𝔯𝔦𝔭𝔱𝔲𝔯𝔢𝔰 Page 46.

Just when you thought you'd seen everything!

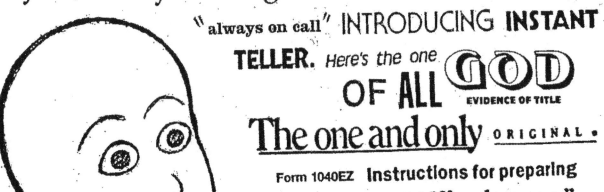

"always on call" INTRODUCING **INSTANT TELLER.** Here's the one OF ALL **GOD** EVIDENCE OF TITLE

The one and only ORIGINAL.

Form 1040EZ Instructions for preparing STRAIGHTFORWARD. **Miracle** WORKING"

This is about tha only
yours to use AUTHENTIC

portrayal OF

The INSTANT TELLER,
you stand to gain by.
'*Revelation*'

The Positive *SPIRIT*
Without *GENDER*.

PROVIDED FOR YOUR PROTECTION.

"All God's children". INNERSOUL SUPPORT SYSTEM !

(Message is Forever.) Many years, many words, from just 1 pen /

DON'T THANK (((Me,))) THANK GOD.

Democracy

page 46 1/2

Tha Buck Starts Here.

♩ RETROSPECTIVELY EVERYBODY WANTS TO RULE ♫
♪ THA WORLD. WHEREBY EVERYBODY SHOULD
ViA THE POSITIVE, INSTRUMENTING THA
REALITY OF GOD'S WORLD...

GOD

(WORKING THROUGH MAN)

SOUL is THE AURA OF ONE'S INNER GOODNESS.
FOR ONLY TRUE LEADERSHIP WOULD ACCEPT
POSITIVE INPUT; THUS DEMOCRACY'S FINENESS HOUR.

QUOTE OF THA MONTH

"What is a friend? A single soul dwelling in two bodies." • ARISTOTLE •

GRECIAN FORMULA Phase 2 "What is a friend?

"A PREDOMINANTLY POSITIVE SOUL, DWELLING IN ONE'S BODY."

SIGNED: DR. Sunday

"When is regulated good sense lost in translation."

HOW TO SAY SOMETHING IN SO MANY WORDS

NOTHING PERSONAL, NATION-WIDE PERSONEL. PLENTY OF UNSUITED FOR MANAGEMENT LOW-LIFERS, WORKING IN HIGH PLACES SEMINAR. METAPHYSICALLY SPEAKING, SERIOUS AS A HEART-INTACT!

Share your views and vision EXAMPLE: WORDS TO LIVE BY!

• NEVER GOING OUT OF YOUR WAY TO BE NICE,
  IS ALWAYS BEING NICE ON YOUR WAY THERE.
• SACRIFICE INCONSIDERATION FOR CONSIDERATION.,
BE PERCEPTIVE WITH THA POSITIVE, PROCRASTINATE THA NEGATIVE
"TO SPEAK KIND WORDS IS TO HEAR KIND ECHOES."

ONE UNIVERSAL GOD Bless you
survivability plus growth
Righteously Combating madness

THIS HERE BEING A 10 COMMANDMENTS REFORM, BY WAY OF A

"" SEVERITY OF SIN EVALUATION. ""

By Tha Numbers Train Like a Pro
IM PRUV ALL Seminar exemplifies
What you need to know AND Process.

FREEDOM OF CHOICE AUTHORIZED BY GOD.

Tha Message that Once Was, Is Not Forgotten!'

1. WAR: (((INSTIGATOR))) ... SELF-DEFENSE IS JUSTIFIABLE....

2. 'SPIT ON THEIR GRAVE' TERRORIST, MASSMURDERER, SERIAL KILLER ...

3. MURDERER: = (THOU SHALT NOT KILL.) ...

4. GREED: SELF-INDULGING PROFESSIONAL MISMANAGEMENT OF MONEYS OR POLICY MAKERS,
   ARE THA DIRECT OR INDIRECT CAUSES OF ONE BEING SENTENCED TO LIFE OR DEATH,
            BY WAY OF FINISHING LAST IN THA HUMAN RACE ...

5. PREJUDICE: PEOPLE THAT DON'T ENJOY LIFE = HATRED OF OTHERS SPURS GREED...

6. CHILD ABUSE: (SEXUAL, PHYSICAL, OR EMOTIONAL) CHILD PORNOGRAPHY.

7. STEALING: OBVIOUS VERSUS, INTERTWINING UNFORESEEN EXAMPLES:
   LYING TO SOMEONE TO RECEIVE SEXUAL GRATIFICATION, OR PROSTITION BY WAY OF
   MARRYING SOMEONE JUST FOR THA SAKE OF MONETARY, SOCIAL, OR POLITICAL GAIN.
         FALSIFYING A RESUME TO ATTAIN A SUMPTUOUS INCOME.
   THA OVER-ALL ECONOMICS OF IRRESPONSIBLE BABIES HAVING BABIES ...

8. HOCUS POCUS: MIND ALTERING DELUSIONARY DRUGS; " TO MANY CHURCHES AND NOT ♫
   ENOUGH TRUTH." IS LIKE BIG TIME DRUG DEALING AL-QAIDA, CLAIMING TO BE THA
                  MORAL AUTHORITY ..
   ALCOHOL ABUSE. SOBER, OR INTOXICATED LEAD FOOT THOUGHTLESS
   DRIVING HABITS. ABUSIVE, OR IRRESPONSIBLE GAMBLING HABITS ...

9. (ADULTERY. MARRIAGE INFIDELITY: ABUSE OR THA 2ND HAND REPERCUSSIONS
         OF WHO'S BEEN SLEEPING IN MY BED ? ...

10. NON-RECOGNITION OF 'MY REALISTIC BIPARTISAN BILL PROPOSAL;
      INTHAT ONE NEEDS TO ATLEAST GET 25 % OF THA OPPOSITIONS
      PARTY TO SIGN ON FOR BILL LEGITIMACY.(EXAMPLE PROTEST)
      THA EMPTY NEST 2009, 1 PARTY BOGUS, HEALTH - CARE - BILL .
      'EVERY POLITICIAN RUNS THEIR CAMPAIGN ON A SLAM-DUNK
      BIPARTISAN PROMISE, AND WHEN THA REAL GAME STARTS
      THEY CAN'T EVEN MAKE A LAY-UP ...

Judgment Day

ON WITH THE SHOW

'Let's Leave tha Ice Age' **Answers** to "All God's children".

How to Interpret That Heavenly Knowledge !

MARCH 1996 Questions by Reno News & Review, Religion Issue,

☑ Check here if we can use your answers (if we so choose) in our upcoming issue on religion.

3. Do you believe in heaven, hell and judgment day?

Does Compute BY WAY OF REALITY IN THA GRASP OF A LOGICAL SENSE! TO SHARE IN THA REALITY OF <u>HEAVEN</u> ON EARTH IS TO SHARE IN THA INDIVIDUAL RESPONSIBILITY. <u>HELL</u> IS REALISTIC WAR, STEMMING FROM ALL OF THA ATTRIBUTES OF 'PREJUDICE, 'GREED, 'OPPRESSION,'MURDER AND MAYHEM ETC. <u>JUDGEMENT DAY</u>. **Lend Me Your Ears** IS WHEN AN INDIVIDUAL COMES TO "Spiritual" TERMS WITH THESE HERE FOREMOST STATEMENTS.

Powerful Testimony: Message is Forever. '

featuring **MANUSCRIPT** CLONING SCHOOL,

this book will be among your family's most cherished possessions.

PAGE 46 3/4

GOD

The Positive Spirit

They Shall Be Heard

𝔚hat 𝔖aith 𝔗he 𝔖criptures

All roads lead to ↗

"That was tha week that was".

Tha Next Chapter

AMAZING VIEWS
News, notes, quips & quotes
Observations, confessions and revelations

WANTED

New leader, new nation, new world !

BOOK TITLE: TODAY 'i' MUST CONFESS.
ISBN PUBLISHED IN 2008. ISBN PUBLISHED IN 2009.
ISBN PUBLISHED IN 2010, 2011 VERSION PENDING...

A look back YOURS TRULY, (((LEADERSHIP.))) JUNE 5th 2010, AND
COUNTING. " OIL RIG DISASTER " WITH APROX, 2 MILLION GALLONS A DAY EFFUSING,
IN REGARD TO MY PROPOSAL AND PRIOR TO THEIR DEPARTURE I, RECEIVED
THANK YOU LETTERS FROM THA NOW LATE - FREDDY THA FISH, TOMMY THA TURTLE,
DORIS THA DOLPHIN, ALONG WITH PENELOPE THA PELICAN, AND FRIENDS!
= PATIENCE = WORN = DECISION = TIME.
GULF OIL SPILL STOPPAGE SHOW??? DAY 47, YOURS TRULY DECISION; ANSWERS TO:
HIGH-POWERED EXPLOSIVES, STOP THA BLEEDING, KICK POSTERIOR END GAME!!!
'STUCK ON STUPID' IN THIS A CATASTROPHE, IS KEEPING UP WITH THA (JONES LAW.
FURTHERMORE, "PUTTING A 6 MONTH DRILLING MORATORIUM, ON A 'ALREADY
TOXIC GULF SOUP BOWL, IS RIDICULOUS!

· · · · · · HONESTLY SPEAKING · · · · · ·

PRESIDENT OBAMA IS A GREAT GUY, AND HAS A WONDERFUL FAMILY.
IN HIS OWN WORDS! "I DO THINK AT A CERTAIN POINT
YOU MADE ENOUGH MONEY". THINKING OUT-SIDE THA BOX,
THERE IS SUCH A THING AS LIBERAL SALVATION; BY GOLLY,
HE'S GOING TO ENJOY THESE JUSTIFIABLE ECONOMIC QUOTES
ON PAGES 50 & 51, ETC. BY YOURS TRULY, ABOUT BEING A
MODERN-DAY MORAL CRUSADING, FELICITOUS, ROBIN HOOD !!!

IN REALITY, NEW AGE ROBINHOODISM IS NOTHING MORE THEN BUSINESSES MOST DREADED
WORD CALLED = COMPETITION =. THEREFORE IN UNION WITH GOD...

♫ MA-MA, DON'T LET YOUR BABIES GROW-UP TO BE COW'ARDS. ♫

Americans still want people of faith as leaders.

"THEREFORE SINGING IN ACA-PULCO, 'HERE I COME TO SAVE THA DAY."

IA) REPRESENTING AMERICA, ITS IMPORTANT TO HAVE VARYING POLITICAL POINTS OF VIEW. **WHO'S NEWS:** is Door opening for this religious **ACTION HERO** **overachiever**?

story REFLECTION Just Listen To What He's Saying –

Warns against 'political cowardice' of, **or** inaction. **REACH OUT AND SHOCK SOMEONE.** **i condemn**

THA DEMOCRACY OPPRESSING POLITICAL AND MEDIA COWARDS IN THIS COUNTRY RESTING ON THEIR LAURELS AND HARDY, ALONG WITH THEIR INABILITY TO CREATE SOCIOECONOMIC DIGNITY AMONG THA IMPOVERISHED.

BOOK PROPOSED — **TAKEOFF POINT** "responsibility". IT appears THAT WITHOUT A ACTIVATED 3RD PARTY, WHISTLE BLOWING WATCH DOG ENTITY., THA COMMON FOLK TAX PAYER DOLLAR WILL ALWAYS BE SUBJECT TO LOBBIED INSIDER, MAFIA-STYLE- 'WE KNOW WHATS GOOD FOR YOU' EXTORTION!

WHEREAS THIS IS MY IDEA OF A BIG-TIME ELIOT NESS, OPERATION...

Democracy Tha Promised Land

We're interested in what you think

Spoken Here PAGE 48.

LIFE IN THESE UNITED STATES.'

WRITTEN BY **a new high iQ, prophet.**

ARMED WITH THA CONSTITUTION,
VOTER ALERT !
OF THA PEOPLE, BY THA PEOPLE,
AND FOR WHAT PEOPLE?

TO LIVE IN A COUNTRY THAT STRESSES

SO MUCH EMPHASIS ON GETTING THA

TAX-PAYING, BACK-BONE-BASE OF

COMMON FOLK PEOPLE OUT TO VOTE.,

THEN ONLY IN COMPARISON TO HAVE

THA CHUMP-CHANGE--CONTRIBUTING

SUPER-DELEGATES, TRUMP AWAY

ONE'S WINNING IN A POPULAR VOTE,

IS AN ATROCITY OF DEMOCRACY,

OR A CON---STITUTIONAL DISGRACE.

FOR THA MOST PART OF A 300 MILLION,

((CONSUMER))

$ COMPOUNDED TAX-BASE 'UNITED WE STAND...

YOURS TRULY SIGNED, **Customer SERVICE Representative for**

Tha voters nobody seems to know

GIVE US A PIECE OF YOUR MIND
REMEMBER WHEN?

YOURS TRULY, SENT A POST CARD TO FOX NEWS, WASHINGTON D.C. `STATING - FAIR & BALANCED, EQUAL TIME`?

OR HOW TO ENTICE AN ARROGANT CHICKEN INTO A `VERBAL SLAUGHTER HOUSE! FOX NEWS SHALLOW AS A MUD PUDDLE. UNFAIR AND UNBALANCED., "YOU GUYS CAN'T HANDLE THA TRUTH." POST CARD IN REGARDS TO `ALL THOSE YEARS OF COVERING UP ON MY SENT FORTH NEWS - WORTHY POSITIVE, CONSTRUCTIVE CRITICISM., YOU KNOW EXACTLY WHO I AM ! - THEREFORE I DON'T EVEN NEED TO SIGN THIS ...

"FOX NEWS N.Y., TURNED OUT TO BE JUST AS UN-ACCOMMODATING."

Your Feedback Is Important

PAGE b 49

June 2007, BOOK'S 27TH ANNIVERSARY

WHAT GIVES, GUYS?

In my words 'Tha pursuit of happiness is nothing but a — Con—stitution.'

NATIONWIDE

ALL ONE BIG SUE CITY IOWA

AMERICA

" THA MINIMUM WAGE LAW. IS NOTHING MORE THAN A FANCY NAME FOR SLAVERY."

IN OTHER WORDS SAFARI AS I KNOW. IF YOU UNEARTHED THA FOUNDING FORE FATHERS AND ASKED THEM IF THEY EVER OWNED ANY SLAVES? THEIR RESPONCE WOULD HAVE BEEN ! "WERE YOU REFERING TO OUR EMPLOYMENT OF MINIMUM WAGE WORKERS?" **reform plan-**

A REVOLUTIONARY PREACHER'S **mind** is a terrible thing to waste ➡

Educational Backround:
YOUR QUESTIONS ANSWERED

I WAS A STRAIGHT Ⓐ STUDENT, IN JIM CLASS ! Take Note *Writer* of **CREATED** *EMOTIONALLY* **EQUAL ETC.** Founder of **THE POSITIVE** Faith Religion. **Heavenly Knowledge uniquely qualified in a league of his own;** *SCHOOL REPORT CARD!* **Send in tha Clowns** — *WAS A HIGH SCHOOL AND COLLEGE DROP OUT, WHEREAS HE* **NEVER** *QUITS DOING HIS HOMEWORK.* **NERD Power** *SIGNED, I WAS A GEEK MYTHOLOGY MAJOR.* (**A How to Int-erpret example**) *DID MY THESIS ON THA SIMALARRY.T'S BETWEEN BILL GATES, AND STEVE FORBES.* **Whassup!**

"New system In Defense of Modernism"

THA PROPHET, THAT BELIEVES IN PROFIT SHARING. **stockholders** 1985 NEWS*BRIEFS "CAPITALISTICALLY *SPEAKING, AS FOR EVERY BUSINESS 'I OWN OR INFLUENCE, HENCE FORTH LOGO; 50 PERCENT OF ALL BUSINESS PROFITS WILL BE CATEGORICALLY SHARED BY ITS EMPLOYEES."* $$$ provocative new insights on **Sports** $$$ How High Is Too High? Math Made Easy *THRU ACCOMPLISHMENTS NOT EXPECTATIONS, MAKING MONEY THA OLD FASHION WAY! SIGNED: SANTA CLAUS, BECAUSE I'M THA ONE WHO KNOWS HOW TO PUT A JUSTIFIABLE (CLAUS) IN EVERYONE'S CONTRACT.*

WINNING A WAR OF WORDS

(Closing tha Case on <u>GREED</u>) Page 51.

Survival A big motivating factor

Report from tha Front

NATIONAL AFFAIRS

victims get their day in court.

To tha rescue

THE LAW

The Positive SPIRIT, long reach:

did you know THA SPECIFIC DEFINITION OF <u>GREED</u>

IS ANY PERSON <u>HAVING OR WANTING</u>

<u>MORE THAN</u> WITHIN A LIFE TIME

THA 'REALISTIC NECESSITYS OF

"<u>CHOICE</u>" IN FOOD, CLOTHING,

SHELTER, TRANSPORTATION,

NEEDLESS TO SAY MEDICAL

ATTENTION, INTHAT MAN'S PLIGHT ALONE

IN LIFE IS ATLEAST WORTHY ENOUGH

TO COVER ALL THA MINIMAL.

written in (1983) DR. SUNDAY AND THE BOSS, CHALLENGING ONE'S CONSCIOUSNESS...

Nobody beats him in blame game!

FEBRUARY, 1992 IN AS FAR AS NATION-WIDE HEALTH

CARE IS CONCERN! WITH THA GOVERNMENTS

LACK of SYMMETRY, WE'RE ALL THAT

MUCH CLOSER TO THA CEMETERY."

POINSETTIA And THEN SOME...

THA AMERICAN DREAM, OR THA RIGHT TO THA PURSUIT OF ~~HAPPINESS~~ ECONOMIC DIGNITY -STIMULUS PACKAGE!"

IN REFERENCE TO ALL MY FELLOW DIRT POOR, BE IT MALE OR FEMALE COLLEAGUES, THAT COULDN'T LIFT A CURVE TO ALL! I DO BELIEF THAT THERE IS A YOUR OK, I'M OK, FAIR PLAY FORMULA APPROACH TO THIS SITUATION! BY WAY OF TAKING OUT A 10% TAX ON EVERY EMPLOYES DAILY TOTAL SALES RING-UP., ALONG WITH A — YOU NEED TO REPORT YOUR TIPS ON THA BACK OF A TIME CARD-ETC-THAT ARE ANYTHING OVER A YOURS TRULY, $75. TAX FREE 'B, TIP PROPOSAL!

QUALITY OF GOOD SERVICE INCENTIVE FACTOR, OR BUST. HAVING ME SIGN A NIGHTLY TIP SHEET REPORT, I FEEL THAT THA UNITED STATES GOV.- IS A TOTAL DISCONNECT TO ME. WHO ARE THOSE GUYS ANY WAY? IN THAT I'M NOW JUST WORKING FOR THA (I.R.S.). FORGET CLUELESS, PRIORITIZED WITH THA MIDDLE CLASS OBAMA, OR McCAIN,. I WANT TO KNOW WHO'S RUNNING FOR PRESIDENT OF THA (IRS)?" MANY YEARS AGO WHILE HE WAS STILL IN OFFICE, I WROTE TO ~~THA~~ ~~FATHER~~ BUSH, AND HE NEVER WROTE BACK TO THANK ME., THEN EARLIER THIS YEAR I WROTE TO THA SON BUSH, AND HE NEVER WROTE BACK TO THANK ME. SO NOW WHAT YOUR DEALING WITH-RIGHT HERE IS ~~THE~~ HOLY GHOST, WORKING THRU-ME TO LET YOU ALL KNOW, OR PROOF THERE OF ABOUT THA REALISTIC LEGITIMACY, OR RECOGNITION OF "ALL GOD'S CHILDREN". PERSPICACIOUSLY, FAITH BASED INITIATIVES FINENESS $ HOUR. IN PERSPECTIVE OF "PARADISE & POVERTY." LIVING WITHIN THIS A PLUTOCRATIC SOCIETY; IN THAT THA 'MINIMUM WAGE LAW, IS NOTHING MORE THEN A FANCY NAME FOR SLAVERY...

IN CONCLUSION, CLINGING TO MY RELIGION WITHOUT ANY GUNS, VOTE FOR ME SIGNED — RUNNING FOR DOG CATCHER,. **Whassup** DOG!

Americans are fed up with **Calling for Justice**
GO BEYOND DREAMING
time for honesty arrives WITH **Common**
Sense philosophies on ISSUES
IN OTHER WORDS 2ND NONE FAR AND AWAY

MORE FOR YOUR MOOLA

A Little Help
From a Friend **on** Economic concerns:
CHECK THA MILEAGE. PAGE 52.

writer's
MARCH 3, 1995 **POINT OF VIEW** on Social Security
KEEP IT SOLVENT FOREVER., TRUST ME!

ANYTHING LESS WOULD BE UNCIVILIZED...

Bail 2008 (((FINANCIAL CRISIS))) 2008 Out
WHAT THA --- HELL --- IS GOING ON ?
KARZAI FOR CAR-CZAR, SOUNDS ASININE? SO DOES THIS 2008, BAIL-OUT FIASCO.
Y-O-U- NEED ME, (((VERSUS))) BAIL-OUT THA TITANIC.
" IN THA HUMAN-RACE, THA PRIORITY OF EDUCATION IS A MORAL ONE."

(((((GREED IS NOT GOOD.)))))
"PAR FOR THA CURSE" IN THA NEWS--50B$ SCAM ARTIST,
MAD-OFF-AND WE'RE NOT GOING TO TAKE IT ANYMORE.
2008: AUTHOR'S NOTE, SMART MONEY: ALL THESE SURE-THING INVESTORS
SHOULD HAVE HAD AT LEAST 250 THOUSAND SECURED, IN F.D.I.C.
BANK DIVERSIFYING; BEFORE THEY EVEN CONSIDERED GETTING INTO
ANY KIND OF A FILTHY RICH INVESTMENT SCHEME. MORAL OF THA STORY--
-DON'T TRY LIVING BEYOND ONE'S OWN REALISTIC WAYS AND MEANS COMMITTEE.

"" BEER SUMMIT "" JULY 2009 , CAMBRIDGE CONTROVERSY: (LIFE IS PSYCHOLOGY);
"NEVER COP AN ATTITUDE WITH A COP"
NO MATTER IF YOU'RE BLACK, OR WHITE.
EDUCATIONALLY SPEAKING, STATEMENT HAS
THA POTENTIAL OF SAVING PRIVATE CITIZENS MILLIONS...
SIGNED: KING ME

WHAT DOES YOUR FUTURE LOOK LIKE?

TIME CAPSULE—What ever happened to spoken 'for tha good of tha country' _{PAGE 52½}

Are civil rights in jeopardy?

Questions EARLY *SPRING* 1991 **By** 🌐**USA WEEKEND**

Share your views and vision on equality for tha '90s

fill out this important survey and mail it back to us.

OK'

If you could Identify ONE STEP OR POLICY TO BEST IMPROVE CIVIL RIGHTS

BY THA YEAR 2000, (IT COULD CONCERN FUNDING, BUSING OR EDUCATIONAL REFORMS, POLITICAL CHANGE, ETC. WHAT WOULD IT BE ?

` YOURS TRULY, RELIGIOUS EDUCATIONAL REFORM:

Tha big picture

"Tha Purpose OF Life" _{on PAGE 24}

God THE 'POSITIVE, SUB-CONSCIOUS-PEOPLE- **whisperer**...

ALONG WITH ="PRAYER OF THA TRAFFIC JAMS AND JELLIES"(ETC) --- BE THAT THERE IS A THIN LINE BETWEEN A 'GENIUS AND A IDIOT, IN THAT 'PATIENCE IS THA KEY; WHEREBY 'THE POSITIVE IN HUMAN --- KIND, CORRELATES INTEGRITY...

PUBLIC INTEREST AMERICA'S TO-DO LIST **RIPE FOR JUDGEMENT**

TWITTER BATE: JAN.2011   'WEEKLY TV, REPORT **ANYONE**???

MY FAVORITE CZAR IS --- WHEN'S THA LAST TIME YOU'VE HEARD ANYTHING ABOUT THA AUTHORITIES TAKING THA REALISTIC BULL BY THA HORNS IN TORT REFORM, MEDICARE AND MEDICAID
                                        FRAUD???

-- (NEAT FREAK) --   (ETC)

"(gODLINESS IS) ONE'S MORALLY PRIORITIZED (CLEANLYNESS)!
        'NOW GO TAKE OUT THA GARBAGE...

WIDE-EYED AND FOCUSED I'LL NEVER FORGET THAT SUNDAY MORNING WHILE WATCHING THA TV NEWS, AND HAVING BREAKFAST., THA METEOROLOGIST FORECASTING 175 MILE AN HOUR WINDS, THAT ARE HEADED STRAIGHT TOWARDS NEW ORLEANS, AND DUE TO LAND IN APPROXIMATELY 24 HOURS, FROM NOW! 'KNOWING THAT AND THAT, THA LEVEE'S WERE ABOUT AS SAFE AS, A ALL-TERRAIN MARATHON RUNNER ENTERING A RACE WEARING CARD-BOARD FLIP-FLOPS., — I KNOW MYSELF I, WOULD HAVE ATLEAST BATTEN DOWN IN BATON ROUGE!

forcasting **TAKEOFF POINT:** UPON 1ST ALERT, ANITA — HUMUNGOUS CONVOY OF BUSES READY TO GO!

AFTERMATH HELICOPTER OBSERVATION: IN REGARDS TO ALL OF THA PEOPLE THAT WERE STRANDED AT THA CONVENTION CENTER ETC. —'GROUND CONTROL TO MAJOR TOM! WE ANITA — MASSIVE AERIAL DROP OF FOOD, (MRI's) WATER, PORTA-POTTIES, ETC.

Spreading tha Blame?

" 'BLAME IT ON THA BOSSA-NOVA! POSITIVE RAIN, NEGATIVE RAIN, ATMOSPHERIC POSITIVE, ATMOSPHERIC NEGATIVE. CREATIVE CURRENTS! 'BLAME IT ON THA RIO DE JANEIRO, FALSE GOD, SON-WORLD, WORSHIP EXHIBIT! "

A Straight Look at **story** REFLECTION

Answers to NO. ▶ We DON'T NEED ANOTHER STATUE ROUTINE, IN THAT TO <u>MOUNT</u> OR <u>RUSH</u> <u>MORE</u> CELEBRATED IDOLS ALL THA WAY THRU CROSS WORSHIP OF A STRUCTRED MAN. THUS IN CONCLUSION " SAY CHEESE". Reality Check

Ⓖⓞⓓ, ONLY PICTURED US HERE...

IN BRIEF: War on Drugs

POINT OF VIEW

1989 **Like A Version** PAGE 54. policy remains firm.

Tha Look-Ahead Factor *That Won't Go Away*

((<u>NEVER EVER</u>, <u>NEVER</u> <u>LEGALIZE DRUGS.</u>))

" <u>LEGALIZE</u> HARD CORE, 'CARD CARRYING' DRUG <u>ADDICTS</u>" IN A CONTROLLED ATMOSPHERE AND <u>TAKE A REAL BITE OUT OF CRIME</u>.

FAR TO MANY INNOCENT <u>VICTIMS</u> HAVE BEEN <u>ROBBED</u>, <u>BEATEN</u>, OR <u>KILLED</u>. TO APPEASE THEIR HABITS- 'WILL YOU BE NEXT? <u>INCESSANTLY WHY</u> <u>MUST SELF-SERVING CLIFF</u> JUMPING WASTED (LIFE) HOLD PRIORTY OVER, <u>RESPECTABLE</u>?

Sanctions BY THE BOOK etc. ★★★★★★★ (1994)

Congress has acted ★★ now it's your turn.

((BOGUS POLICY)) <u>TARGET</u>: TO REPRIMAND "WANT FOR NOTHING, COULD CARE-LESS" GLOBAL LEADERS. <u>RESULTS</u> FROM WORKING HOME-BASE SUPPLIERS TO CUSTOMERS. <u>ONLY</u> THA LITTLE PEOPLE SUFFER...(BOOK'S OPINION) IN NO WAY SHAPE OR FORM, DO I - LEND SUPPORT TO ANY KIND OF WALK-OUT STRIKE; MAY I SUGGEST " WEARING A DATED ARM BAND" IN PROTEST WHILE STILL WORKING; EVEN IF IT TAKES 10 YEARS, TO SEATTLE...

WE NEED YOU AT THA FRONT!
Patients' rights bill approved

IS THERE A DOCTOR IN THA HOUSE? NO. PROBABLY BECAUSE THEY ALL WANT TO GROW UP AND BECOME TRIAL LAWYERS THAT CONTROL THA DEMOCRATIC PARTY! BY WAY OF HANDING OUT HUMONGOUS LAW SUIT PAYOUTS TO PATIENTS, THAT IN RETURN WILL SKY-ROCKET HMO, PREMIUM COST, OR MAKING COVERAGE SO UN-AFORDABLE THAT YOU'LL ALL WIND UP HAVING TO FEND FOR YOURSELF. ON THIS ISSUE I, STAND FAR TO

BACKS BUSH ON:
TORT REFORM & 2007 REVISED PATRIOT ACT... THA **right.**

Gun Digest 2001 Senate backs Bush plan to **end** federal gun buyback program   PAGE 54 1/4

Rapid Fire Giveaway THERES ALLWAYS SOME ACCESSIBLE DUSTY OLD GUN, SITTING AROUND WITH NO INTENSIONS OF EVER BEING USED AND THEN, SOME HIGH SCHOOL KID GETS SAND KICKED IN HIS FACE, AND DECIDES TO RETURN TO SCHOOL WITH VENGEANCE! — AND THEN AGAIN ON SOME BROKEN HEARTED LOVE DISTRAUGHT SOUL, OUT THERE ETC, THATS CONTEMPLATING SUICIDE. ON THIS ISSUE I, STAND FAR TO THA **left.** for DO I SMELL NECESSITY A 3RD PARTY, ANYONE **?**

Mr. President
There's more to us than just taxes. ⟶

"OBAMA-NOMICS"

AUGUST 15th, 2009

PART 1.
(HEALTH CARE)
= RESPONSE
PAGE 54½

WHERE WE ARE NOW

CAMPAIGING THRU A CONCRETE JUNGLE WITHOUT A CONCRETE HEALTH CARE BILL, WILL NOT BE AN EASY TASK. SO LIKE A GOOD PATRIOTIC VOLUNTEER WITH INFO; I DECIDED TO SUM UP HIS 14,000 PAGE BLA, BLA, BLA, TIE-DOWN READ, WITH NO TIME FOR PERSONAL EXERCISE BILL. (VERSUS) EVOLUTION — MY 2 PAGE, HAVE A NICE DAY ESSAY.

FIRST OFF, IS THERE A CEILING IN HIS BILL FOR TORT REFORM. (OUTRAGEOUS LAW-SUITS.) BECAUSE INSTRUMENTALLY I BELIEVE THAT THIS WAS THA ROOT CAUSE OF HEALTH CARE PREMIUMS GETTING BLOWN OUT OF PROPORTION IN THA FIRST PLACE. WHEREAS IN HIS BILL, SHOULD IT GET PASSED - WHAT'S TO STOP THA GREEDY INSURANCE AGENTS FROM UPING THA ANTE ONCE THIS GET'S STARTED, AND TOSSING US ALL INTO A MASSIVE SOCIALISTIC HEALTH CARE GRID-LOCK. INSURANCE CZAR ANYONE? FINALLY EVERBODYS FAVORITE.

QUESTION: IF I, GO TO WORK FOR SOME SMALL BUSINESS, SLAVE LABOR EMPLOYER, AND GET INTO THA SYSTEM, AND THEN EITHER QUIT MY JOB, OR GET FIRED DOWN THA ROAD; DOES MY EMPLOYER GET STUCK WITH MY ON GOING HEALTH CARE PLAN FOR LIFE? THANK YOU. QUESTION: WHERE'S THA 2 MILLION, NEW DOCTORS AND NURSES, THAT ARE GOING TO SERVICE ALL THESE 47 MILLION PEOPLE, THAT WILL BE COMFORTABALLY ENTERING INTO THA SYSTEM?

"CHANGE WE CAN ALL BELIEVE IN" - AS A SHOVEL READY VOLUNTEER.
AUTHOR'S NOTE: IN A CHAOTIC SOCIALISTIC SOCIETY, I'M A PRETTY GOOD UN-LICENSED SHRINK; YOU CAN TELL BY WHAT YOU'VE BEEN READING HERE. I'M GOOD AT DEALING WITH THA YOUTH IN ASIA ORDEAL — AS LONG AS THEY DON'T ASK ME TO EAT SUCIE WITH THEM.

QUESTION: "I KNOW HE'S BIG ON DISEASE PREVENTION" AND IF THIS IS TO BECOME A SUCCESSFUL PLIGHT, WERE GOING TO NEED FULL DENTAL HEALTH CARE, ALSO; IS THERE ANYTHING LIKE THAT IN THAT BILL? IF NOT THIS WILL BE EQUIVALENT TO THA MAJORITY OF US SWIMMING AROUND IN A SHARK INFESTED POOL WITH BLEEDING GUMS. "FURTHERMORE WITHOUT ANY CONCRETE ANSWERS WERE ALL GOING INTO THAT POOL!' AND FINALLY: PAR FOR THA CURSE, WILL CASH FOR CLUNKERS EVENTUALLY TURN INTO BECOMING CASH FOR BODY PARTS? IN CONCLUSION: I JUST HOPE THAT THERE'S NOTHING IN THAT BILL THAT STATES ANYTHING ABOUT PULLING THA PLUG ON DEMOCRACY...

WHAT'S IN STORE? Common $ense $olution Answers to ➡

Vintage health care debate : PAGE 55

IN-BRIEF:
1996. REVOLUTIONARY HEALTH CARE, PROPOSAL BY YOURS TRULY.

(PSYCHOLOGY) WITH THIS NEW UP IN COMING OBAMA, CARE! JOBS ANYONE?

WAIT AND SEE HIRING RESPONSIBILITY $ PROGRAM CREATES ECONOMIC UNCERTAINTY !

THEREFORE DR. SUNDAY **'Mission possible'** HEALTH CARE

PROPOSAL "WITHOUT/ ROCKING THA STATUS QUO BOAT."

THIS HERE BEING A STIMULUS PACKAGE 'LONG TERM EMPLOYMENT BONANZA! "THINKING OUT-SIDE THA BOX" THA GOVERNMENT WITH OUR CON-GLOMERATED TAX BASE, SHOULD INVEST IT IN 'THA GIFT THAT KEEPS ON GIVING'. INVEST IT IN OPENING UP 2 CASINOS IN VEGAS; 1 IN RENO; 1 IN CHICAGO; 2 ON THA EAST COAST, AND 1 DOWN SOUTH! ""TAKE ALL THA PROFITS FROM THOSE ENTITYS AND USE THEM TOWARDS HEALTH CARE VOUCHERS FOR THA NEEDY"... WHO'D EVER THINK THAT THA PATRIOTISM THEME WOULD BE THA BIGGEST NEW DRAWING CARD FOR VEGAS, ETC...

FURTHERMORE BY LAW, HAVING NO LODGING FACILITIES, A LIMITED SNACK BAR, AND GAMBLERS HAVE TO PAY FOR THEIR DRINKS; THUS SUB-CONTRACTING ALL THA CASINO ENTRY-LEVEL WORKERS.

P.S. BUSINESS AS USUAL? - THEY COULD ALWAYS SKIM MONEY OFF THA TOP FOR MEDICARE, ETC. IT'S ALL GOOD; AS THIS "GAMBLER PHILOSPHY" STORY STANDS "REPEL THIS OBAMA CARE, EDSEL" ...FOLLOW-UP ON PAGE 79

Religious Science training program :
Next up on Tell-all book
debate on immigration APRIL, 06'

exemplifies What you need to know **AND** Process.

TAKEOFF POINT : First step, close tha borders.

'IF AMERICA WERE A BLEEDING PATIENT — THA FIRST THING WE'D DO IS TO TRY AND STOP THA BLEEDING!

Do you support a guest worker program? YES. BRIEFING **example :**

or WE'D PAY 5 TIMES, THA AMOUNT WE NOW PAY FOR EACH PRODUCE ITEM. RESTAURANT PRICES WOULD SKY-ROCKET; AND VEGAS WOULD TURN INTO ONE BIG GIANT COBWEB,ETC... 4 YEARS LATER APRIL, 2010 FOLLOW-UP; LAST PAGE IN THIS HERE CHAPTER IS VENTURE CAPITALISM, OR DIVERSIFICATIONS FINEST HOUR...
(((REAL REFORM DEPENDS ON)))

Who has tha best blueprint? ⟶

Experts agree that tha loss of undocumented workers would rock state's economy.

Should businesses be held criminally liable for hiring illegal immigrants? NO.

Uncover tha real truths about

QUALITY OF personal LIFE BRIEFING

EXAMPLE: $ HIGH COST OF EDUCATION ! MANY, MANY, A PROPRIETOR
IN THIS COUNTRY HAVE PUT THEIR CHILDREN THRU COLLEGE ETC; BY
WAY FROM THA PROCEEDS OF THESE HIRING PRACTICES ...

AN HISTORIC Hispanic American

YOURS TRULY mission PROPOSED reform plan.,

--- ON CINCO DE MAYO, I'D CHANGE THAT CELEBRATORY DAY AND REFER TO IT AS
HISPANIC HERITAGE DAY, COVERING A MUCH WIDER RANGE OF PEOPLES." $

Founder of THE POSITIVE Faith Religion.,

Guidelines: "PEACEFUL 'EVOLUTION, REVOLUTION,
IS THA SOLUTION TO BE FREE OF MENTAL POLUTION."

"LIVING IN THIS 4-RACIST NATION. THERE IS NO
'HISPANIC, REVEREND SHARPTON, OR JACKSON,
THAT HAVE MEDIA ACCESS IN 4 HEART BEAT!"

Tha COURAGE TO COME FORWARD ?
AS A BABY GROWING UP I WAS SO TUFF - MY PACIFIER WAS
THAT OF A JALAPENO PEPPER.

WRITTEN BY **A 3rd party, minority overachiever**

SO WHERE'S MY FREE - HOLY'S - PARISHIONERS ??

SIR-CUS = SIR-CUS, or SOMETIMES

MI CASA = OUT LOUD WHEN THERE'S NOBODY ELSE AROUND. -

Specializing in commonsense 'Plan for Prosperity?

ATTENTION EMPLOYERS total overhaul of system ???

LINGUISTICALLY SPEAKING: IF WE EVER WENT TO WAR WITH MEXICO
AND THEY WON, AND TOOK OVER OUR COUNTRY = I'D BE LEARNING HOW
TO SPEAK FLUENT SPANISH LONG BEFORE THA SMOKE EVER CLEARED ...

"MAKING SENSE OF THA CENSUS, OR
ALOT OF PERCENTAGEWISE CATCHING UP TO DO."
THA LANGUAGE HERE IN THIS BROCHURE APPEARS
TO BE MISLEADING TO ME! THEREFORE, I'M GOING
WITH THIS AS IS RESPONSE. " I CONSIDER MYSELF
TO BE A MULTICULTURAL WHITE, HISPANIC. ☒
I LIVE INSIDE A HOUSE WITHIN A COMPOUND. IN-
SIDE THAT HOUSE THERE'S 6 NONRELATED, 'DISCRETE'
MALE FULLTIME RESIDENTS RENTING INDIVIDUAL
ROOMS., PLUS MYSELF, ALL OVER 50 YEARS OF AGE.
'LIKEWISE OUTSIDE THERE'S 4 SMALL APARTMENTS,
3 OF THEM OCCUPIED BY INDIVIDUAL WOMEN, OVER
40 YEARS OF AGE., TOSS IN THA FINAL UNIT BY AN
OVER 50 YEAR OLD, MALE. TOTAL Occupancy 11."
     IN RETROSPECT, THIS OVERALL PICTURE
SEEMS TO 'DELETE THA REALISTIC BIG PICTURE
OF A TOTAL HISPANIC HERITAGE COUNT! IN OTHER
WORDS A SO CALLED 50 MILLION AMERICANS,
OUT OF 300 MILLION, MAY NOT BE ANY-
WHERE NEAR A JUSTIFIABLE ACCURACY.,
TURNING THIS HERE ESSAY INTO A PROTEST!
     ALONG WITH THESE RACIST PERCENTAGE EXAMPLES:
THA TEXAS, TEXTBOOK WARS, SHORTCHANGING OF
HISPANIC CREDITABILITY. THA WINTER OLYMPICS
LACK OF ANY KIND OF HISPANIC PARTICIPATION.
VIEWING THA ENTIRE ACADEMY AWARDS PROGRAM, THA
ONLY HISPANICS I SAW OTHER THEN J-LO, WERE THA
BUSPEOPLE AND THA KITCHEN HELP... SIGNED :

'NO AMERICAN LEFT BEHIND'

Dynamic duo working partners, *message.*

The book A PRODUCT OF A **SUPERCONNECTED** MAN,
AND HIS ⊙Ⓞ Ⓓ! ^{APRIL, 2010} statements put on paper.

APRIL, 2010
OPINION

I.Q. YOU IN ON THIS A YOURS TRULY, FREE-B CONTRIBUTION,
INFO-PROPOSAL: CAN YOU SAY 'YOU HAVE A LEGITIMATE PLAN
THAT CAN SOLVE ALL OF THA UN-EMPLOYMENT PROBLEMS IN
THIS COUNTRY? NO!

'I CAN...

<u>IN-BRIEF</u>: **"My Fellow Americans; Read Listen and Win!**

TAKEOFF POINT FIRST AND FOREMOST, WE NEED TO MAKE
ENGLISH AS OUR PRIORITIZED OFFICIAL (JOB PRIORITY)
SPOKEN LANGUAGE! proposal COURSE OF STRATEGY- make ^{THEN}
MEXICO, OUR 51ST STATE. DROP THEIR LONG STAND-
ING $ DEBT TO US, OR FORWARD IT TO THA MURDEROUS
LOW-LIFE, DRUG CARTEL TO PAY BY MONDAY MORNING,
TO KEEP US OUT OF TOWN. ALL NEW AMERICAN MOVE-IN
CURRENCY MAKES FOR $+¢. OFFER MEXICO'S PRESIDENT AND
HIS POLITICAL ASSEMBLY, A HELPING HAND GOVERNORSHIP
FOR THA FIRST 4 YEARS, TILL FREE ELECTIONS CAN COME
TO TERMB. OVER-ALL THIS HERE BEING A WIN, WIN,
BETTER QUALITY OF LIFE FOR MOST, PROPOSAL! KEEP IN MIND
BECAUSE OF THA WARM CLIMATIC PARADISE, THA PAY
SCALE WILL BE FOR THA MOST PART, ON THA CHILLY SIDE!
THEREFORE STILL KEEPING THA BOARDER CLOSED
FOR THA FIRST 4 YEARS, WILL GIVE OLD SCHOOL AMERICANS
MOVING IN, A CHANCE TO SET UP SHOP WITHOUT ANY CHAOS.
P.S. AN INITIAL BI-LINGO WINDFALL?

P.S. (((FLUENT ENGLISH ANYONE?))) WHEN ALL THESE NEW AMERICANS ARE
APPLYING FOR 'GOOD PAYING JOBS IN THIS COUNTRY, THEY'LL ALL BE GETTING
ASKED TOUGH QUESTIONS FOR IT LIKE = WHO'S JOE BIDEN ???

Crime & Punishment

Tha Next Chapter

AMAZING VIEWS

News, notes, quips & quotes

Observations, confessions and revelations

WELCOME TO RELIGIOUS AND POLITICAL SUNDAY SCHOOL:

SO WHO'S THA DEVIL?

♫ EVERYONE THA DEVIL INSIDE! ♫
INTERNAL FREEDOM OF CHOICE,

CAN BE A POSITIVE MORAL RESPONSE

BY SOMEWHAT OF A HARMLESS PUPPY;
((EVERTHING IN LIFE TO A DEGREE.))
AS OPPOSE TO,

TURNING ONESELF INTO A DEVIL-AWFUL,
FLEA-BITTEN, RABIDUS PIT-BULL...

SIGNED: POOCH PAWSITIVE,

COLD NOSE TRAINING A MUTT MUST.

DIAL **Ext.** K-9, AND ASK FOR KEN - NEL ...

Guidelines: AS HEAVEN WOULD HAVE IT - REPEAT AFTER ME
1,000 TIMES; THOU SHELT NOT INSTIGATE KILL... ⟶

(((EXAMPLE))) "*WITHOUT THA MEDIA-BANNED, READILY AVAILABLE PROPAEDEUTICAL RHETORIC, OF DR. SUNDAY; THIS TRANSGRESSIVE MONSTER— ETC-ETC-ETC-WAS CREATED IN THA GOOD O'L U.S.A.*"

1/11/11 NATION-WIDE *Letters to tha Editor* ETC.

'POLICE STATE TAX-PAYERS, IF WERE HAVING FUN YET???
" TUCSON TRAGEDY SHOOTER, HAD NO VISUAL 'DOMINANT,
POSITIVE' HEROES, OR MENTORS IN HIS WORLD! INTRODUCING
BIG TIME MEDIA MUZZLED, DR. SUNDAY 'LEADER OF THA
MUZZLE'M FAITH SOCIETY; THUS 'LITERACYS FINEST HOUR.
 * STRAW THAT BROKE THA CAMELS BACK? QUESTION BY
SUSPECT LOUGHNER, THAT NEVER GOT ANY AUTHORITIVE
RESPONSE! LOUGHNER: "WHAT IS GOVERNMENT, IF WORDS
HAVE NO MEANING?" * DR. SUNDAY: RECOGNIZABLY TANGIBLE
GOVERNMENT, THEREFORE 'BECOMES GENESIS TO THA CREATION
OF PROFOUND, CONSTITUTIONALLY ACCOUNTABLE WORDS OF
MEANING! THANK YOU...
(IN THA WORDS OF JOB - GET A JOB!)

'SOUL SEARCHING SUSPECT' = SOMETIMES I FEEL LIKE A
NUT, SOMETIMES I DON'T. THA DIFFERENCE BETWEEN
LOUGHNER BEING CALLED CRAZY, AND THA POLITICAL
PARTISAN BLAME FINDING FAULT FINDERS, IS THAT
LOUGHNER DID HIS TALKING WITH A GUN! INSTANTIATING,
ONCE THAT FIRST AMMO CLIP GOT EMPTIED THEY ALL
WENT TO SUBSTANTIATING JARAD'. --- AND I BET
ALL MY CHRISTIAN ILLUSIONIST READER FRIENDS,
WERE EXPECTING ME TO SAY SOMETHING LIKE
— LOUGHNER, WAS A PRACTICING SPACE CADET WHO
SHOT CONGRESSWOMAN GIFFORD, BECAUSE HER HUSBAND
WAS A RIVAL ASTRO'NUT! 'A TEACHABLE MOMENT
ANSWERS TO: "NOT EVERYONE IS LOCK STEP
DANCING TO THA BEAT OF SO CALLED ORGANIZED DEAD
PULSE RELIGION! THEREFORE THA OPPRESSIVE
GOVERNMENT & MEDIA'S ROAD BLOCKING OF 'MY
RELIGION = COULD BE THA MISSING LINK THAT
COULD HAVE SET 'HIS SOUL SEARCHING
DEMEANOR FUNCTIONAL"...

C H R O N I C L E S PAGE 57 WITH A KICKER.

America's Most Wanted:

(PRAYER of THA AFTER THA FACT SOCIETY.) In Testimony Whereof

GOD, DIDN'T PUT US ON THIS HERE EARTH TO KILL ONE ANOTHER. STATE of MIND, FRAME OF MIND. NO STATE OF MIND IS PERMANENT!

If you ignore -it,- it will go away., IN THAT Reader's CAN DIGEST THIS STANDARDIZING OF ONE'S INTELLIGENCE!

"WHEREAS PATIENCE IS THA KEY!"

VICTIM'S OUTRAGE

"ALL MURDERERS SHALL BE SET FREE."

HELL'S ESCALATION, OR REHABILITATION CITY IS A TOWN WITHOUT PITY. SO LET ME HIP YOU BEFORE WE SHIP YOU... IN FUTURE WORLD GAMES LET A MURDERER SWIM HOME FROM THA MIDDLE OF THA OCEAN TO PROVE THEIR NOT UNJUST PRE-MEDITATED, SPONTANEOUS, INSANE DEATH CER-TIFICATE HOLDERS, BUT INCOMPETENT SWIM-MERS THROUGH NO FAULT OF THA SYSTEM. IN CONJUNCTION, THA SHORT CHANGING OF A IGNOMINIOUS ONE'S LIFE EXPECTANCY., TENACIOUSLY DOING UN TO OTHERS FOR THA GAMES MUST GO ON.

PEOPLE BURGERS MY FAVORITE!

SIN-FULLY DELICIOUS

Facing Down tha Monster

LEAVE YOU WITH ONE SIMPLE THOUGHT:

YOURS TRULY, BEING THEIR WORST NIGHTMARE!

TIME AND TIME AGAIN I REALIZE I'LL, HAVE A TOUGH TIME IN TRYING TO PASS THESE CRIME BILLS; BUT THEN AGAIN NO REST FOR THA WICKED IS LIKE OWNING A PIECE OF THEIR MIND; THA WORRISOME PART ! 'INTERPRETATION OF A BIBLICAL MYSTERY TURNAROUND? 'TO THEM - " I 666, WILL BE THA MOST HATED MAN IN HISTORY." P.S. ON THAT CRIPPLED, FORT HOOD MAJ. HASAN, GUY ; INSIGATOR OF CRUEL AND UNUSAL PUNISHMENT TO THA INNOCENT. I'D PUT HIM IN A HUGE BATH TUB OF WATER UP TO HIS CHIN. - 'O BY THA WAY JUST DON'T GET SLEEPY ...

Crime & Punishment

Examining Tha Death Penalty

Scriptures *Suffering From Some Ailment ? (1983)*

Year in Review PLANNING FOR TOMORROW'S GENERATION

WITHOUT IDEOLOGY THA PURPOSE OF LIFE?

CRIMINALS ARE READ THEIR GLAMORIZED PREDETERMINE CATERED LEGAL GAME RIGHTS, WHEREAS THEY ALL HAVE THEIR GLAMORIZED PREDETERMINE CATERED LEGAL RIGHTS, TO BE GAME CRIMINALS ! **They did a bad, bad thing** FOCUS ON behavioral freedom to RAPE MUG SLUG BUG DRUG, THRILL KILL PILL OR PLUG. WAR WHORE SEXUALLY EXPLORE, OVER NIPING RECKLESS DRIVERY, BRI—BERY ALL AT THA EXPENSE OF SOMEONE ELSE'S.

VICTIM'S OUTRAGE

ONE-UPMANSHIP report is only beginning of debate

RELATIVE TO ALL RELATIVES UNJUSTICE IS UNSOLVED CRIME, WHEREAS THA VICTIMS DO INSURMOUNTABLE TIME, FOR EVERY FORM OF CRIME IS UNJUSTICE STATE OF MIND, IT'S PEOPLE BORN OF GOOD INTENSIONS THAT NEVER SEEM TO RHYME, TO WALK A CROOKED ROAD IS A LIFE OF WASTED TIME.

A reality check of

What They Dodged forecast

PAGE 57½

Tha Funny Professor With a Heart big

IN FACING REALITY HERE ON PLANET EARTH LIKE IT OR NOT, WE'VE ALL BEEN GIVEN AN INEVITABLE DEATH SENTENCE!

expanding intellectually FEATURES

("SYNCHRONIZING OUR MORAL COMPASS.") *Solution*

focus is on oppressed freedom

of RELIGIOUS thought —

answers to ♪ **Give'em** some of **that**

'**new-time religion!** IN BRIEF
Critic's Notebook June 2001

HOUSTON: A Mother is <u>accused</u> of drowning her five children.

—AFTERMATH! <u>DELIBERATELY FOCUSED WHEN IT CAME TO USING THA TELEPHONE TWICE</u>, THEREFORE SHE SHOULD HAVE BEEN OUT WORKING SOMEWHERE AS A TELEMARKETER.

Classified Dept. **TELEMARKETERS NEEDED** on-target bonuses. Must be self-motivated ...

<u>SAME CASE SCENARIO</u> **(MAY-'03)** Speaking Her— <u>Mind</u>, IN REFERENCE TO THA DEVIL IN THA DETAILS, WOMAN IN TEXAS THAT MOST RECENTLY STATED "<u>GOD, TOLD HER TO KILL HER OWN CHILDREN.</u>"

①<u>The</u> <u>Positive Spirit</u>, Ⓖ Ⓞ Ⓓ,

— 'DOES NOT SUGGEST NEGATIVITY.—

IN REGARDS TO ONE'S CONSCIOUS OR SUBCONSCIOUS, THOUGHT PROCESSING!

analyze *wiser* Biblical **dialogue** Correctness

PAGE 58 'Reloaded' Follow-up On NEXT Page, MORE THEN ONE-WAY TO SKIN A <u>**CAT**</u>ASTROPHE!

CHAPTER ON CRIME: Take a university class credit without being admitted to a university.

nation wide, LETTERS TO THA EDITOR:

Head-to Head, Here's tha skinny on tha unabomber 'Nutcracker' trial.

"WATCHING ALL THOSE KIDS RUNNING AROUND BEAR CHESTED IN SUB-FREEZING TEMPERATURES AT A FOOTBALL GAME AND I'LL TELL YOU, THEY'RE ALL CRAZY. THA MAJORITY OF US LAW BIDING TAX PAYING CITIZENS THAT FOCUS AT A PAY STUB EVERY WEEK WILL TELL YOU THAT THA GROSS PAY IS GROSS, OR INSCRIPTIVELY CRAZY. — "IN REFERENCE TO HIS ACTIONS HE, WAS NOTHING MORE THAN A MAD AT THA WORLD HARMFULLY CRAZY, INTROVERTED, SELF-CENTERED TEED-OFF RECLUSE; SUCCUMBING TO ONE'S OWN HATRED OR BITTERNESS. SURREALISTICALLY THA 'DEVIL REACTING WITHIN THA DEFENDANTS OWN NEGATIVE SEED OF THOUGHT SUGGESTIVE SUB-CONSCIOUS,. SUGGESTED TO HIM TO DO IT — AND HE THAT IS OF ONE'S OWN FREE WILL! CHOSE TO DO 'CONSCIOUSLY AS SUCH". POINT BEING, YOU'D HAVE TO BE CRAZY (NOT) TO PRINT THIS MANIFESTO"...

Not there yet?

'LEGACY'

DON'T RE-WRITE THIS DIARY!

STATEMENT OF

"ALL GOD'S CHILDREN"

INITIATING

INDIVIDUAL

RESPONSIBILITY?

FACTS SAVE LIVES!

" WORLD FUTHER SOCIETY $;

'PAGING ALL THOSE NON-OPPROBRIOUS,

NON-ABRASIVE, ACTION HEROES

OF HEAVENLY INSTANTIATING

CREDIBILITY

ANYONE!"

COMMUNITY EDUCATION

RECREATE
YOURSELF.

NEXT UP: A Straight Look at story REFLECTION ▷

JULY 2011,. RACIST (77) MASS-MURDERING NORWEGIAN, WAS A ONE SUPREME 'SON WORSHIPING CHRISTIAN. (VERSUS) 'MY MEDIA MUZZLED MINISTRIES, "ALL GOD'S CHILDREN" RELIGION.

APRIL 2007; MEDIA TELEVISED

IN-PUT ON THIS CHO-SEUNG-HUI GUY, THAT COMMITTED THA VIRGINIA TECH MASSACRE! THIS CHOICE INTROVERTED SOCIETAL MISFIT, WAS SUFFERING FROM PROSPERITY ENVY., BEING A CHARM-SCHOOL DROP-OUT PSYCHOPATH, HE SHOULD HAVE BEEN SENT BACK HOME FOR GOOD, TO WORK AN 80 HR. WORK WEEK, IN HIS PARENTS DRY-CLEANING BUSINESS. ((THA STRAW THAT BROKE THA CAMELS BACK!)) 'OR COMPOUNDING THIS SITUATION IS WHEN HE TRIED TO SOLICIT SEX FROM A — I'LL ONLY DO YOU IF YOUR A HONORARY GRADUATE OF CHARM-SCHOOL ESCORT SERVICE! THEREFORE AFTER BEING JERKED AROUND OR REJECTED, FEELING DISTRAUGHT HE TOOK VENGEANCE., WHEREAS HAD HE BEEN LIVING IN BROTHEL NEVADA, — YOU'LL FIGURE IT OUT!! "DIFFERENT STROKES FOR DIFFERENT FOLKS." IN CONCLUSION HAD THIS EVIL-DOER EVER HAD THA CHANCE TO READ MY BOOK, (FOR SOME A NEW AGE LITERARY EXORCISM) HE MIGHT HAVE BEEN ABLE TO SNAP OUT OF HIS NEGATIVE MIND SET, AND FORESEE HIMSELF WITH A POSITIVE AMEN.

NEXT IN A SERIES HE FINDS OUT HIS, SPIRITUAL FATE. — **Awake-up call.➔**

Next up on Tell-all book:

On terrorism, **Understanding tha Problem – so called experts see no easy answers.**

In Testimony Whereof ACCOUNTABILITY

'SHOW ME THA MONEY, Democracy; Public Has No Say!

Lecturing FEATURES **Take My Advice, Please.**

STORY CLOSE-OUT DETERRENT PROPOSAL WRITTEN IN **1999**, by YOURS TRULY.

1ST STOP, SOME OF THA MOST RECENT **Chain of consistency examples** HISTORY OF DOMESTIC TERRORISM.

NEWS OF RECORD on THIS DEC. 24, 2008 BRUCE PARDO,

Santa shooter Unveiled: SEEING INTO tha BRAIN! I CAN SHOW YOU SOME 17, MILLION PEOPLE, THAT N-E-V-E-R HAD 17,000 DOLLARS IN THEIR LIFE, AND NEVER DID ANYTHING AS MEAN-SPIRITED AS THAT! I CAN SHOW YOU SOME 17 MILLION PEOPLE, THAT GOT DIVORCED AND NEVER DID ANYTHING AS MEAN-SPIRITED AS THAT! IN OTHER WORDS WELCOME TO OUR WORLD. MR. — YOU EVIL-DOING EXTREMELY SELF-CENTERED, G-REEDY, MORONIC, DEEP-SEEDED, DEVIL-PROVOKED NEGATIVE SPIRIT **Magnet.**

N E X T. U P NEWS OF RECORD ON THIS GUN TOTING MALL MASSACRE HAWKINS, DEMOND. DEC. 5, 2007. HIS MIND SET! 'I'll be famous'. "KEEP THAT IN MIND." IN REALITY — OVER THEIR DEAD BODIES — HE BLAMED EVERYBODY HE SHOT FOR HIS MISERY + SELF-PROCLAIMED MEANINGLESS EXISTENCE!"

Gone but not forgotten

= THEY WILL BE REMEMBERED; TRUTHFULLY I HOPE!!! =

IN REFERENCE TO THA 7AM, START OF THA NEWS DAY ON
AUGUST 6TH, 2010. (N.Y. NBC TV.)
TALK ABOUT BEING TOTALLY CLUELESS OF
♫ I'M LOOKING AT THA MAN IN THA MIRROR ♫

"IN REFERENCE TO THIS SCHEMEOLOGICAL LYING, THIEVING,
MURDEROUS, LOW-LIFE SLIM BALL SCUM BAG, INTHAT THIS
(GIVE CREDIT WHERE CREDIT IS DUE!) CONNECTICUT DISCONNECT,
WHO WISHED 'HE COULD HAVE KILLED MORE OF THOSE WHITE
PEOPLE HE WORKED WITH, BECAUSE THEY WERE A BUNCH OF RACIST!
GEE, THEY HIRED HIM DIDN'T THEY?
RIGHT THEN AND THERE, IN A GRAND CENTRAL STATION SECOND;
'WITHOUT ANY 'TV REBUTTAL FOLLOW-UP FROM 'HIS STATEMENTS.
THIS ALL CAME OFF AS SOUNDING LIKE SOME KIND OF SYMPATHY
SUPPORT FOR HIM BEING JUSTIFIBLE IN THESE KILLINGS.
-END OF STORY- IT'S ALL GOOD- GET ON WITH YOUR DAY!
= THEREFORE POSITIVELY ENRAGED =
I GUESS I'LL JUST HAVE TO SPEAK OUT FOR THA DEAD;
IT WON'T BE THA FIRST TIME!
THIS HERE BEING A TEACHABLE MOMENT.
THERE'S AN EXTREMELY 'LIMITED AMOUNT OF REASONS THAT
WARRANT KILLING ANOTHER PERSON; AND RACISM FOR RACISM SAKE,
DOESN'T APPLY!

IN CONCLUSION: THIS PREMEDITATED PSYCHOPATHIC PERPETRATOR,
WAS A REAL WOLF IN SHEEPS CLOTHING 'EPITAPH WORTHY' RACIST!
HUMILITATED FROM BEING CAUGHT STEALING AND FIRED;
HEARTLESSLY HE BECAME A 'REVENGE TAKING RACIST.
FINANCIALLY HE HAD A DREAM JOB THAT THA MAJORITY
OF AMERICANS WILL NEVER SEE THAT KIND OF A PAY SCALE.
IN OTHER WORDS WORKING THERE YOU COULD HAVE CALLED ME, RABBI-TACOBENDER,
AND I WOULD HAVE LAUGHED ALL THA WAY TO THA BANK.

—— AND DON'T GIVE ME THAT WHITE GIRL FRIEND ROUTINE;
"THERE'S 90 MILES OF DIFFERENCE BETWEEN FREE RANGE BOOTY CALL = EASY SEX =
AND LOVE; AND HAD 'HE HAD THAT KIND OF A LEARNED INTUITION,
MOST LIKELY 'NONE OF THIS WOULD HAVE EVER HAPPENED!"
HISTORICALLY, MANY A RACIST SLAVE OWNER MADE THAT SAME
KIND OF FIMILIAR SEX IS SEX, BOOTY CALL...

"SPOTLIGHT ON RACISM"

HIGHER EDUCATION STARTS WITH HIGHER INTELLIGENCE.

Welcome to tha Neighborhood

"FOLLOW-UP ON PAGE 74½

Terrorist **PREVENTION** Clinic

NEWS OF RECORD on **Columbine** school shootings, **tragedy.**

1999, A Look At ThΛ Evidence.

MALICIOUS HIGH SCHOOL SHOOTINGS IN LITTLETON COLORADO, ETC. <u>IN SEARCHING TO FIND THEMSELVES THESE TWO CULPRITS</u> BASKING IN THEIR HATRED AND PREJUDICE, <u>WERE SUFFERING FROM INTELLECTUAL GROWTH SHUT DOWN.</u>, THUS HIGHLY QUALIFIED AVENUES TO ACHIEVE ONE'S MATURE POSITIVE DEVELOPMENT ARE BEING ROAD BLOCKED BY A NATION

Searching For Closure !

ThΛ End Is ≡

THA INFAMOUS DYLAN KLEBOLD'S, TAPED RECORDED FAREWELL CRUEL WORLD, FINAL STATEMENTS ! "<u>I KNOW I'M going TO A BETTER PLACE THEN</u> ≡ **Here.**"

BIG TIME, KEEP THAT IN MIND AND PLEASE READ ON !

'revolutionary crunch time' or Same **Old** story, different day ?

NEWS OF RECORD on **Religious 'extremists'** !

Example On '*Global*' terrorism COMBO, *exemplifies* What you need to know **AND** Process ▶

Fort Hood victims
Tales of war,
take center stage

NEWS OF RECORD: two stories **one cause.**

project story BRIEFING **in** Response **to**

MOMENTS IN HISTORY

Americans must not allow
'old soldiers' to fade away

"THA BEGINNING OF"

MARCH, 2003 A Nation at War **OPERATION IRAQI FREEDOM**

` U.S. soldier held in fatal attack with grenades

on **My fellow Americans** HOW OTHERS SEE US

` IF I WERE A COMMANDING GENERAL, I'D PARACHUTE
THAT TREASONOUS SOLDIER, ON A ONE MAN MISSION
INTO THA HEART OF BAGHDAD, TO CAPTURE SADDAM
INSANE! SPECTRALLY — SIGNED BY" GENERAL PATTON
Me, ON THA BACK." March Madness ETC.

Scripture   = KIND OF =
` THE WILL,, paves way for a new leader.

of "SATAN'S LITTLE HELPERS" IN NEED OF SHOCK-THERAPY!

brain-dead CAVEMEN

'Bad to tha Bone'

PASS THIS SIMPLE I.Q. TEST

(((HISTORY REPEATS ITSELF)))

TO UTTER THA WORDS "G-OD IS GREAT" THEN TO PRECEDE AND KILL INNOCENT PEOPLE TELLS ME, THAT THESE EVIL-DOERS ARE STRONGLY DEVOTED TO SERVING SATAN, OR IF YOU WILL **godzilla**.

Your **GUIDE TO** Addressing tha Problem.

DOCTOR'S BOOK OF NEW World **REMEDIES**

"profiles in courage" **Tha DOCTOR is in.**

**M I S S I O N
S T A T E M E N T**

All God's children

THEIR DIRECTION IN LIFE

INVITATION **shows 'OUR** Side is

"UNITED THRU POSITIVE DEEDS AND ACTIONS."

ENLIGHTENING VIEWS

CHART YOUR COURSE TO a Better

improvement OF **INTERNATIONAL** history

" NEW-AGE SPIRITUAL GROWTH REVIVAL "
By Founder of THE POSITIVE Faith Religion.
"B.L.T. SANDWICHES FOR EVERYBODY"

WHAT WOULD MOHAMMED HAVE DONE?

HOMERUNS, TOUCHDOWNS, ETC. CELEBRATORY FINGERS POINTING UPWARD IN APPRECIATION TO GOD, WHO'S ALL GRACIOUS AND GOOD!

RECOGNIZABLY OPPROBRIOUS; ONE CAN ONLY MURDEROUSLY KILL, IN THA HIDEOUS NAME OF GODZILLA, SATAN, OR THA DEVIL. 'READ 'EM AND WEEP' BLASPHEMOUS RADICAL ISLAM, POST MOHAMMED? ONLY TRUTH CAN FREE YOU! TO HAVE ACCEPTED THA GOOD FORTUNE OF EVOLUTIONARY ADVANCEMENTS, SUCH AS IN GOING FROM EVERY DAY CAMEL RIDING RUSH HOUR, TO RIDING IN 4 AIR-CONDITIONED CARS, TO HAVE GONE FROM BIRD WATCHING - TO FLYING IN A BIG BIRD. ALL THA MODERN DAY AMENITYS ALONG WITH ADVANCED WEAPONRY, EVERYTHING FROM THA LATEST IN MINE FIELDS, TO BLOW YOUR MIND RELIGIOUS FIELDS!

ELUCIDATING 'PRIORITIZED MORALITY, IN THAT YOU KNOW YOUR STILL LIVING IN THA MORALITY STAGNANT STONE AGE, WHEN EATING BBQ RIBS IS MORE SINFUL THEN KILLING A MEMBER OF ALL GOD'S CHILDREN. DEFINITELY THIS HERE I-MUMMY EXPRESS, IN NEED OF A BIG TIME OUT.

IN RETROSPECT, PROVING TO BE THA GREAT LEADER HE WAS-MOHAMMED, 'WOULD HAD OF APPROVED THIS MESSAGE...

(New age) Religious responsibility Exam!
Get ready for truth support.

WAR on TERROR – ATTACK on America

UNITED BY TRAGEDY – Tha effects of tha terrorist attacks on

SEPTEMBER 11, 2001 'day of infamy.

'A Picture of Gloom'

Face *to* Face a reflection of feelings answer **to** "INSTIGATORS OF HELL" RELIGIOUS FAILING ZEALOTS. 'showcases tha RADICAL ISLAMIC JIHADIST. **tha Rise of Real People** Preaching a Gospel of ANTIPATHY! this HERE DETERRENT proposal BEING A TRUE TO MORALISTIC LIFE, UPSTAGING REALITY CHECK IN PROTECTING THA HOME FRONT. "NOT IN OUR BACK-YARD", will defeat fanatics'. "IN THAT THA ONLY WAY TO WIN **This War** IS TO BRING DOWN THEIR BELIEF SYSTEM." THIS HERE BEING A HOW TO PRESENTATION! →

Writer Author **mourns death** of **innocent.** **Q**TODAY'S **QUICK READ** TRIVIA stirs past

WE ARE PLEASED TO ANNOUNCE THAT

on DNA backlogging PAGE 63

What's News ! Bible revision **Caveman** Extremists **Smoke and Mirrors Roll Over Convention, CLEARANCE SALE.** IN REFERENCE TO **World Terrorism.** THERE iS **NO** HALLELUJAH iN A EVILDOER, THAT'S ON A Mission FROM gODZILLA! `Negative Spirit` To it's core' Has **NO** RESPECT FOR INNOCENT LIFE. `WHAT PART of SATANIC MARTYRDOM DON'T THEY UNDERSTAND? THEREFORE TRY VISION CORRECTION SHOCK THERAPY DETERRENT proposal. **Think!** FACING WEST *****YOUR** CREMATORY GRAVE STONE SHARING ETERNAL EPITAPH WILL BE WRITTEN iN YOUR NAME, FOR SERVICES RENDERED TO SATAN!" (DNA) REMAINS OR NOT—THEY'RE FOR REAL. `SO WE MUST BE. DOMESTIC GUNMAN gONE WILD **Justice at Last.** AUTHOR'S iNSPIRATIONAL RESPONSE `WE WILL BURY YOU!'

Quotable Quotes, Word Power Points to Ponder, HERE AND THERE PREVENTION CLINIC.

"The Art of Restoring Magnetic Heads." PAGE 64

FOUNDERS FILE *starter kit.* READ MY LIPS BOOK!

"Presenting GOD'S INSPIRED WORD."

Big Read "Peace On Earth Sale"

"I BELIEVE YOU CAN MAKE PEOPLE NICE!"

THIS HERE BEING A HOW TO GUIDE!

"CONFRONTING THA INSTIGATORS OF HELL":

AS IS, DOES YOUR FAVORITE POLITICAN SAY
HE CAN STOP TERRORISM IN THIS COUNTRY?

Lies, damn lies ✝ leadership Failure

CHART YOUR COURSE TO

DOCTOR'S BOOK OF NEW World REMEDIES

Daring of Faith 'Exorcism' is fascinating

WHAT DOES YOUR FUTURE LOOK LIKE?

"unforgettable images"

'Shock and awe Realism' 'Showstopper'
Example: Searching For Real Closure!

INTRODUCING - OR AS SEEN ON TV, BEHEADAL INSTRUCTOR AND MASTERMIND OF 911, OR
SLAUGHTERER OF - NO WAY IN ""HELL"" DID ANY OF THOSE PEOPLE DESERVE THAT KIND
OF FATE... DO - UN - TO - INSTIGATORS " KHALID SHEIKH MOHAMMED " MUST SEE TV,?
TOSS THIS LOW-LIFE SLIME-BALL SCUM-BAG, OFF THA TOP OF THA EMPIRE STATE BUILDING;
AND IN RETROSPECT YOU'LL FIND ACTIVATION OF THIS SCRIPTURAL PAGE ....

Terrorist PREVENTION Clinic PAGE 64½

Areflection Time Showstopper

PAGE64ANDTHENSOME.

DANCING SHEIK TO SHEIK.

`A RADICAL ISLAMIC JIHADIST, UNCONSCIONABLE
MINDSET = IS TO KILL ALL THA INFIDELS;
THEN TO UPSTART A SHIITE (VERSUS) SUNNI, FINAL
SOLUTION WAR! CLUELESSLY EVOLVING INTO A
SATANIC CELEBRATORY `I KILLED 'em ALL END GAME.
NEW DIRECTION ANYONE? REPENT, WITH
A CAREER MAKEOVER TO **THE POSITIVE.**

Birds & Tha Bees

Tha Next Chapter

AMAZING VIEWS

News, notes, quips & quotes

Observations, confessions and revelations

THINKING OUT-SIDE THA BOX! " PAGE 66, PROPOSAL."
DESPERATE TIMES CALL FOR DESPERATE MEASURES., IN THAT
THA END RESULTS FAR OUT WEIGH THA STATUS QUO...

$\longrightarrow$

lifestyle OnAssignment

OR MARRIED to my VOCATION.

process clarify / obligation with God., meets with clients. meets with unlimited.'A EVERY DAY intimate LOVING RELATIONSHIP is a matter of Having adequate time! (First draft of An event is born) true PREPARATION Can find a place for Love and Romance In This a BUSY LIFESTYLE! Who's Tha Right One For You ? Help Wanted: needed A Unique COVER GIRL Attraction with 'Adaptation' of turning into A Multitasker LIVE-IN SECRETARY-MAID and then some ., 'Can you hear me now? WHAT NO TAKERS ? RENO NEVADA, He's not worried-Go for plan B, backup project Proposal! as 'Apt lawmakers debate next CHAPTER ▷

"Tha World According to a LEGALIZE Prostitution proposal"

"HOW TO: BALANCE THA FEDERAL BUDGET DEFICIT,—'AND THEN SOME!
BY WAY OF A ALL-STATE, NATION-WIDE FEDERAL GOVERNMENT CONTROLLED,
((OWNED & OPERATED)) OPERATION OF LEGALIZED PROSITUTION. WHEREAS
THIS SHOULD BE AN EASY DECISION FOR ALL THOSE POLITICANS THAT HAVE
BEEN SCREWING US AROUND FOR YEARS WITH ALL THOSE UN-JUSTIFIBLE TAXES!"

"STEMMING FROM THA WAR BETWEEN THA SEXES."

learning from tha past: a study in history

Thanks for tha memories

NO, DON'T GET ME WRONG. I'M NOT TRYING TO CHANGE ALL THOSE *Fool* CAN'T CATCH ME, SHALLOW LOW SELF-ESTEEM GAMES PLAYED BY THA EVERY DAY WOMEN OF SOCIETY! PLEASE DO. I'M ONLY TRYING TO COMPENSATE FOR THEM! *Nobody's Fool* PLEASE DO LEGALIZE PROSTITUTION **All things being equal.** BEHAVIORALLY SPEAKING, OR VENGING ONE'S FRUSTRATIONS AND HAVING **NO** OUT-LET FOR, IT'S TIME TO FACE ALL THA UNLAWFUL EMOTIONAL AND PSYCHOLOGICAL SPIN-OFFS, SURROUNDING THIS HERE LONG IN THA TOOTH ISSUE.

GIRL OF THA MONTH CLUB, OR RICHTER SCALE

LYING ONE NIGHT STANDS;

Uncover tha real truths about abortion

CRUCIAL POINT HAS BEEN OVERLOOKED:

"**bullseye,** MANY AN ABORTION WOULD HAVE NEVER TAKEN PLACE!"

STUDIES INDICATE PUT AN END TO SEXUAL HARASSMENT IN THA WORK PLACE.

WHEREAS THIS PROPOSAL WOULD GIVE EVEN A **dark side of life** RAPIST AN OPTION. ⟶

defining mission a must read

GUIDE TO Addressing tha Problem.

System needs overhaul! **Tha DOCTOR is in.**

Never Ending **Gender War** PROFILES TRUCK-LOADS OF
ON GOING DISHONEST NATION-WIDE, STORY EXAMPLES:

First stop: Genoa **Loves Me. Loves Me Not.** Story!

MUCH THOUGHT WENT INTO tha Susan Smith, child-murder case.

DOCTOR reports flaws in Saab Story. GO WITH

THA FLO **Anonymous LOVERBOY** Set up WEEKEND **Hot BED**

HONEYMOON scheme. Then *After* Production, made excuse

YOU'VE GOT KIDS. that and *Break Away* **MESMERIZED** Susan Smith.

Wake-Up Call. there is a Cure for "Playboy's Ecstasy"**!**

Hey, wait a second, 'Don't forget' **Scandals:** 1995. Senator **Packwood's Decline and Fall.**
RESEARCH **HIGH-PROFILE** *TAIL HOOK* **CASE.**

issue persist, **come to terms** WITH

THA OVERALL DIGNITY OF A BILL CLINTON.

A **SHOCK & STRUT** proposal WITH A

HAPPIER ENDING. YOU'LL
FIGURE IT OUT.

|HISTORY of politicians *running out of excuses*

ENOUGH. *AS FOR NAMING* ALL *THA REST OF THA POLITICAL*

`BIPARTISAN ILLICIT SEXUALLY IMPLICATED, CULPRITS
90., THEIR JUST LUCKY THAT I, RAN OUT OF PAGE 000 ➡

more Tactics to use in negotiations.

NATION WIDE RURAL-RURBAN Innovation:

NATION-WIDE THERE'S BILLIONS OF LOST UNTAXED REVENUE BEING MADE FROM
ILLEGAL PROSITUTION. GOV. ACCUSED OF SWEEPING SEXUALITY UNDER THA RUG!
FURTHERMORE, CHO-SEUNG-HUI, GUN DOWN 32; TOOK 'REVENGE FROM A NO NOOKIE
FOR YOU, $ ESCORT SERVICE!!! = RODNEY KING'S, INDY 500 RACE WITH THA COPS
'STARTED WITH SOME GAL REJECTING HIS ADVANCES; INTHAT 49 DEAD, FROM RIOTS!!!
GOVERNMENT PROPRIETOR ??? OR STIMULUS program,
THEN JUST PUT 'THIS VENTURE PROJECT, IN MY NAME AND "I'LL FOREVER ANNUALLY
DONATE (ALL) THIS MONEY TOWARDS THA F.B. DEFICIT AND OR, SOCIAL SECURITY"...
(((IF WE DON'T THINK IN TERMS FOR THA GREATER
GOOD OF THA COUNTRY, WE'LL HAVE NO COUNTRY.)))

SEEING THA WORLD THRU THA EYES OF DR. WEARING HEART ON SLEAVE!

MORE GAMES **and War Stories from tha Field.**

····· Vintage Journalism CONTINUED ·····

What's Up, Doc? Soul SEARCHING FOR HELP!

BROKEN HEARTED TO THA MAX,

I'LL GET OVER YOU! test of time, this PAGE 68,

IS MY BRAIN ON HEART-CORE-REJECTION.

BROKEN HEARTS! THIS WAS THEIRS. Suicide SPOUSAL CRIME, ETC.

DRUGS, TRAFFIC FATALITYS, FOR THIS COVERS A 'DEVIL AWFUL

LOT-OF-CEMETERY-GROUND—DID YOU KNOW A BROKEN ♡

= WITH A NOT SO HAPPY ENDING?

proposal for " legalize prostitution " AMERICA!

IN PLEADING FOR THA BROKEN HEARTED MENTALLY
TORMENTED HONEST WAY OF LIVING LIFE STYLE
EMOTIONALLY HANDICAPPED INDIVIDUAL
IN NEED OF SEXUAL THERAPY. In brief
TO BE GODLESSLY GUT WRENCHED OF **a** To Each His Own
OR IN REALITY BY WAY OF THA NEGATIVE SPIRIT,

SATAN

HEART & SOUL

Tha Birds And Tha Bees

'THE gospel According to Word Perfect
'All You Need Is a Match' PAGE 69

"THA REALITY OF TRUE LOVE IS BUILT ON
A POSITIVE ((HONEST)) FOUNDATION."
IN ANY AMELIORATIVE SITUATION,
REFLECTIVELY FOR WHAT IS TRUTH — UNLESS
TWO PARTYS CAN AGREE UPON, YET APPLY TOO.

... And They Lived Happily Ever After

LOVE EDUCATION IS TRUE LOVES GAIN
AND WINNERS OF A Positive FOUNDATION GAME.
JORGE PILLER ASSAULT RELATIONSHIP IN A
BEAST ROW GARDEN OF YE DONE.

blame begins.

Lead us not into Shalt Nots,
UNCIVILIZED ABNORMALITYS ARE
THA CAUSE OF SOCIAL INFORMALITYS.

READINGS FOR REASONING

BREAKTHROUGH TRAINING!

SPECTRALLY, The one and only GOD THE
Positive SPIRIT; is MAN'S GREATEST TEACHER.

Professor's challenge is teaching
TOMORROW IN *Education TODAY*
writes from personal experience

1984 **IM PRUV ALL** Seminar

(QUESTIONS OF THA HEART) YOU Know

IT'S TIME TO START THINKING THAT THERE'S OTHER FISH IN THA SEA, WHEN INSTEAD OF FEELING THA PAIN OF ⇒— CUPID'S ARROWS —→ YOUR ACTUALLY BEING HARPOONED.

Love Education
SEMINAR (a time for reflection) ♥
OVER ALL CompatiBILITY of A

Soul Mate
(Never Say Lie)

playing Positive **Games** 'Shalts and Shalt Nots'

→ STARTS WITH A HONORABLE MATCH, NOT A HONORABLE MENTION, BUT TO MENTION A CALCULATED OVERALL COMPATIBILITY PURSUIT GAME OF CONSIDERATION, TOWARD A BALANCED FLOW of HONEST CIRCUMSTANTIAL TRUTH., DANCING TO THA BEAT OF THE RIGHT DRUMMER IS THA RIGHT BASIS OF A POSITIVE RELATIONSHIP, OR LOVE BOAT WITHOUT SINKING. (((PROGRAMING YOURSELF FOR THA LONG HAUL ?

'MY FAVORITE POSITION WITH A WOMAN IS WHEN I —▷

STOP WONDERING. In This Fine Romance

What Makes Love Last? In Memory of

GOOD OLD-FASHIONED (Affection).

"WHAT'S MORE IMPORTANT THEN SEX IN A MARITAL RELATIONSHIP? ANSWERS TO LONG HAUL AFFECTION SUPPORT, REASURRANCE!"

new book educator spells out vision

All things being equal.

BEHIND THA LINES

knowledge is your best insurance.

'Two Can Play That Game, from tha book of love'.

INVOLVEMENT

INTIMATE LOVE IS NEVER TAKING ADVANTAGE OF THA ONE YOUR INTOMATE WITH, OR SEPERATION OF OWNERSHIP IS DOING FOR SOMEONE, NOT TO SOMEONE .. FOR WHAT IS LESS, IS LESS THAN HONORABLE, OR PAST THA LONELINESS IN A RELATIONSHIP ANYONE!

THEREFORE THA PERFECT GAME MINUS PERFECT PLAYERS, WHEREAS TO LOOK FOR THA HONEST FACE YOU CAN FACE AND BE CLEVER, IS THA HONEYMOON THAT WILL LAST FOREVER ...

SYNCHRONIZED TO Page (—▷) *Romance Is Here To Stay*

((Love On Course))

♥ DEAR _____

LIFE IS A Game, INTHAT AS ♥
Trust IS WRITTEN, THIS IS THA WAY
I HONESTLY FEEL ABOUT YOU., OR
LIKE SWANS YOU HONEY BUN, THAT MATE FOR LIFE!
I BEE-LEAF YOU TO BEE MY COMPLETE
COPYRIGHT VALENTINE, LIFE LONG MATCH.
IF I WERE THA RICHEST MAN
IN THA WORLD, OR POOREST.
IN ALL OF LIVES ENDEAVOR - I'M ATTRACTED
ENOUGH TO YOU - MYSELF - TO - BEE - HIVE
- WITH YOU - FOREVER.
INTHAT I'M A HONEST MAN THATS
FOWL-ing IN LOVE WITH YOU,
THUS A ONE FLOWER MONOGA-
MOOSE' POLLINATOR CLEVER,
BECAUSE I FIND YOU
A REAL TREASURE.
~ Birds And Bees

Signed _____ "

CHARTING A NEW COURSE

playing <u>Positive</u> **Games** 'Shalts and Shalt Nots'

Morals in a biblical tabloid

Adding up tha costs – **Mystique no more!**

EXCRUCIATING, WHEN You Can't Tell tha Players

IN A WORLD THAT HASN'T THA Foggiest

IN IT'S TEACHINGS OF HOW TO ATONE ONE'S

LIFE LONG MATCH THRU CIVILIZED COURTING.

Ah Yes, I Remember Them Well.

book of love 𝄞 ' Setting *Tha* Agenda

Time Well Spent Serving Your Needs

Don't you wish you had seen this ad in 19 – ?

— AND DEAR GOD, According To BOOK'S

OVERALL CURRICULUM, 'NO NEED TO FORGIVE ANY–

ONE NOW; FOR THEY NOW KNOW WHAT THEY DO.'

(((OR PARALLELS BEST ONE–UPMANSHIP.)))

A tale of two testaments comes

alive. Project Community *INDIVIDUAL*

RESPONSIBILITY, **Welcome to tha Neighborhood!**

Thumbs up ready to preach to *Tha* masses

GIVING CREDIT Exceeding Expectations

How do you like me now?

Tha debate over gay marriage "Tha facts."

high court rules

Allowing gays and lesbians to marry legally

"Tha Massachusetts Constitution affirms tha dignity and equality of all individuals. It forbids tha creation of second-class citizens."

"People should not be discriminated against."

Tha panel was adamant that creating a separate, marriage-like institution for same-sex couples would not satisfy tha state's Constitution. _____ *TOTALITARIAN ANYONE?*

Defending tha sanctity of marriage with "3,000 years of recorded history.", "Marriage is a sacred institution between a heterosexual man and a woman." Tha 1996 Defense of Marriage Act, defining marriage as tha union of one man and one woman. Tha law also said individual states were "not obligated" to honor same-sex marriage laws passed in other states. *THA FACTS BY YOURS TRULY, WRITER OF THIS A CIVIL UNION, BEST ONE-UPMANSHIP* **proposal**, *OR STRAIGHT EYE FOR THA QUEER AGENDA!* (strongly worded) *IN RETROSPECT LET A SAME-SEX MARRIAGE LICENSE, BE DOCUMENTED IN PRINT AS A UN-TRADITIONAL MARRIAGE LICENSE* PAGE 73

YOURS TRULY, *WITH THA WISDOM OF A KING SOLOMON!*

As Good As It Gets, becomes A rally point

As history unfolds, a textbook keeps up.

LESSON **PLANNER** RECOGNITION.

— *IN AS FAR AS TRADITIONAL* marriage *GOES!*

" *WE MUST PROTECT THIS* institution."

set tha record straight.

Signed Founder of "THE" POSITIVE Faith Religion.

THA CHANGING FACE OF *It's All Good*

NO DEFENDING THA CAVEMAN—"LIFE BEGINS AT 50!"

LONELINESS is cutting off your ear, AND NEVER getting discovered.

LONELINESS NEVER HAS TO WORRY ABOUT THA LIFE EXPECTANCY OF EFFORTLESS FORE PLAY, NOR A SPOUSE THATS OUT HAVING AN AFFAIR. THUS LONELINESS NEVER PLAYS ANYBODYS FOOL, OR MEAL TICKET... LONELINESS AT HOME, COMES AND GOES WITHOUT ANSWERING TO ANY PERSON... PERSE LONELINESS NEVER GETS V.D, HERPES, AIDS, OR NEEDS AN ABORTION CLINIC...

PAGE 74.

LONELINESS IS NEVER BEING A PARENT HAVING TO EXPLAIN WHY YOU BROUGHT THEM INTO THIS WORLD OF UNFAIRNESS... SIGNED ANONYMOUS, LONELINESS ALWAYS SIGNS THAT WAY...

BOOK TITLE: TODAY 'i' MUST CONFESS.
SUBTITLED: A SALESMAN FOR GOD,.

There comes a TIME in **LIFE** when you've got to Reader's Digest **Newsweek** AND accept a few things.

HIGHWAY TO HEAVEN

Here's Lookin' At You! ▶

SMILE! STRAIGHT FACED RELIGION, IS STRAIGHT JACKET RELIGION.

THA END IS ~~NEAR~~ HERE !!

READ MY BOOK.

FRIAR FLYER

Who Speaks For God ?

MOSES DID , WITH 'THE TEN COMMANDMENTS, ETC. ETC.

Who Speaks For God ?
Need a new roommate
In Testimony Whereof
GOD

'THE POSITIVE SPIRIT, GHOSTWRITER.

INNERSOUL SUPPORT SYSTEM ,.

THIS BOOK SPEAKS VOLUMES ...

"SPOTLIGHT ON RACISM"

THA CLEAR THINKING COMMON GROUND OF ONE'S HAVING
INTELLIGENCE, IS SITUATIONALLY BEING ABLE TO
ACKNOWLEDGE, OR DETECT --- EXAMPLE: GOOD COP, BAD COP;
GOOD WHITE MAN, BAD WHITE MAN; GOOD BLACK MAN, BAD BLACK MAN;
GOOD PIT-BULL, BAD PIT-BULL; ETC, ETC, ETC. A TEACHABLE MOMENT?
WHEREAS 'THICK-SKINNED' ETERNAL OPTIMISM, IS HOW ONE FINISHES
FIRST IN THA HUMAN RACE. SIGNED:DR.SUNDAY, HOORAY FOR OUR SIDE...

Up to tha Challenge, Sportsline :

Tha Next Chapter

AMAZING VIEWS

News, notes, quips & quotes
Observations, confessions and revelations

A big league lesson in caring. A clear path of action 'Americanizing GAMES, We can build one America?

Insider *Sports* proposal., **Diversify** *OUR SAFETY AND LESSEN GLOBAL INTENSITY.*

'writing revolution' On record FOR THIS 1984 OPINION proposal

story REFLECTION Meter Is Running.

deliver us From RETHINKING **LIFE ON MARS**

COMPETITION

EXPANSION

PROFESSIONAL

BASEBALL FOOTBALL BASKETBALL HOCKEY

Take me, please Page 75

project helps AMERICAN individuals find work.

employment expected to surge

With New faces for **winning mix** !

history improvement

CHART YOUR COURSE TO INTERNATIONAL INVESTING

STOCK MARKET SUMMARY Open Ownership Door

BUY - SELL - TRADE . Hip Yankee's spend big bucks.

A new World Public Auction proposal →

True Redemption.

Tuesday, March 31, 1992

"YES! WE'RE A RARE BREED US SPORTS FANS A GOOD PORTION OF US REJECTED PROFESSIONAL ATHLETES AND COACHES FOR ONE REASON OR ANOTHER, BEING PERFECT MOMENTUM CHANGING TIME OUT WIZARDS, ARM CHAIR QUARTERBACKS, AND PITCHING CHANGE EXPERTS.

I'LL ALWAYS RECALL MY MOST INSPIRATIONAL MOMENT IN SPORT. THA 1976 NCAA FOOTBALL NATIONAL CHAMPIONSHIP GAME. SPORTSCASTER KIETH JACKSON. "CATHOLICS VERSUS PROTESTANTS, NORTH VERSUS SOUTH, NOTRE DAME VERSUS BAMA. THESE ARE THA WARS THAT WERE MENT FOR MANKIND." HAVING NO FAITH IN MYSELF AND ONLY IN THE GOD I SERVE, THAT STATEMENT WAS ONE OF MY GREATEST COMMUNIONS IN FORMULATING MY IDEOLOGY TO THA REALITY OF UNDERSTANDING MANKIND.

WORLD SERIES, OR WORLD SERIOUS. BRIEFLY, HOW MANY CUBAN AND SOUTH AMERICAN BASE BALL PLAYERS AWAIT THESE SAME OPPORTUNITYS. $HOW MANY ASPIRING SANDY KOUFAX'S DO WE HAVE IN ISRAEL, OR ROCK THROWING KID'S IN THA GAZA STRIP THAT COULD, PIECE OF CAKE THROW RICKEY HENDERSON OUT AT SECOND. $HOW MANY PERSIAN OR RUSSIAN WEIGHT LIFTING MEAT HEADS, DO WE HAVE THAT COULD PUT A LAWRENCE TAYLOR ON HIS BACK IN PROTECTING A QUARTERBACK etc.

PEACE ON EARTH?

THA FAMILY THAT PLAYS TOGETHER, STAYS TOGETHER.

WRITTEN BY: AT ONE TIME AN ASPIRING FOOTBALL COACH THAT CAME TO REALIZE IN THA REAL GLOBAL FIELD OF PLAY, THAT THA WHOLE STADIUM COULD USE SOME GOOD COACHING ...

BOWLING for Justice, NO EXCUSES
New proposal right up bowlers' alley

COLLEGE FOOTBALL CAMPAIGN national CHAMPIONSHIP PLAYOFF ?

FRUSTRATING College football Bowl picture Conclusion clears up Max,

with Free Speech PROPOSAL OF A 1993 RANKINGS SOLUTION .

INITIALLY WRITTEN 1993 (CAPSULE EXAMPLE) PAGE 76½

FOLLOWING A 10, GAME REGULAR SEASON SCHEDULE ENDING ON THANKSGIVING WEEKEND. A CONSENSUS OF THA TOP RANKED 16, TEAMS SQUARE UP IN A ELIMINATION PLAYOFF, BY WAY OF UTILIZING ALL OF THA BOWL LOCATIONS, OR ROTATING THA NATIONAL CHAMPIONSHIP GAME EACH YEAR TO BE PLAYED ON OR ABOUT, THA 15TH OF JANUARY, IN A WARM OR DOME STADIUM.
MUST SEE TV!

SCHEDULING THESE PLAYOFF GAMES TO BE PLAYED IN THA MONTHS OF DECEMBER AND JANUARY, INTHAT TO SHOW BACK TO BACK FINAL 4 GAMES, SOMETIME IN JANUARY WOULD BE APPROPRIATE, AS OPPOSE TO THA STATUS-QUO CRAMMING THEM ALL IN ON NEW YEARS DAY TO SOME HUNG-OVER HALF-ASLEEP, TV GAME SWITCHING BUG-EYED VIEWING AUDIENCE, LET ALONE THA WASTED ADVERTISING DOLLAR.

CONTROVERSIAL CALL SOLUTION ANSWERS TO BY WAY OF USING THA INSTANT REPLAY CAMERA IN THESE HERE PLAYOFFS! GOING BACK TO SCHOOL, PRO-FOOTBALL COULD LEARN ALOT FROM ADOPTING THA PRESENT DAY EXCITEMENT FROM A COLLEGE →

PLAYOFF POSSIBILITIES TODAY IN SPORTS HISTORY Follow up on Next page

"NO EXCUSES, `NO CRYBABIES".

— ▷ JUSTIFIABLE OVERTIME GAME FINAL SCORE SCENARIO. STRATEGIC COMPOSURE! PRO FOOTBALL COULD ALSO LEARN ALOT FROM A `LATE GAME 1ST DOWN AUTOMATIC CLOCK STOPPAGE.

story REFLECTION Meter Is Running.

HAD ENOUGH System needs overhaul!

Public backs agenda

1993 RANKINGS EXAMPLE OF MATCH-UPS)

#①. FLORIDA ST.(VS)#⑯ COLORADO - ALOHA BOWL
#②. NOTRE DAME (VS)#⑮ MIAMI - LAS VEGAS BOWL
#③. NEBRASKA (VS) #⑭ ALABAMA - PEACH BOWL
#④. AUBURN (VS) #⑬ BOSTON COLLEGE - FIESTA BOWL
#⑤. FLORIDA (VS) #⑫ TENNESSEE - COPPER BOWL
#⑥. WISCONSIN (VS) #⑪ OHIO STATE - ALAMO BOWL
#⑦. W. VIRGINA (VS) #⑩ ARIZONA - CITRUS BOWL.
#⑧. PENN ST. (VS) #⑨ TEXAS A&M - HOLIDAY BOWL

WITH VICTORS ADVANCING TO BOWL GAMES SUCH AS GATOR, SUGAR, LIBERTY AND FREEDOM.
(ALWAYS THA HIGHEST RANKING TEAMS MATCHING UP WITH THA LOWEST.)

PAIRING FINAL 4 TEAMS AT THA ORANGE AND COTTON BOWLS, ALONG WITH THIS YEAR JUSTICE GOES WEST TO THA ROSE BOWL SITE FOR NATIONAL CHAMPIONSHIP GAME. Story and *moment is frozen in time.*

Looking Back `got game? SIGNED: BIG FOOT BALL FAN ...

OPINION ON NASA `space shuttles`

ECONOMIC PRIORITIES! OTHER THAN SATELLITE COMMUNICATIONS ETC, DON'T EXPECT TO GET A WHOLE LOT OF SUPPORT $ FROM YOURS TRULY., UNLESS NASA GOES FUNKY AND NAMES THA NEXT SPACE SHUTTLE SOMETHING LIKE "RICH MANS TOY." PRIVATE ENTERPRISE-THEY'RE CALLING YOUR NAME. Written by A FORMER BEACH FRONT PROPERTY SALESMAN FOR MARS. MORALLY SPEAKING **Shattering beliefs** NOBODY TAKES OFF THEIR SPACE SUIT AND GOES SKINNY DIPPING. NOR DO ANY WOMEN WEAR TWO PIECE SPACE SUITS. SHORING UP, THIS IS A BEACH WHERE THA SHARKS ARE THA ONE'S THAT ARE SELLING ALL THA PROPERTIES. Legislature PAGE 78

Say "Farewell to" Poorly thought out budgets.

GETTING A WORD IN EDGEWISE.

lessons from An Outsider's Inside Moves

Commentary ON Terminal Care:
Too Painful, Too Prolonged

OPINION ON DR. JACK KEVORKIAN'S assisted right-to-die

'Politically corrected' "TERMINAL MERCY." IN THAT I STAND IN FAVOR OF, AS LONG AS WE GET A 2ND QUALIFIED DOCTORS OPINION! THIS WAY WE CAN ALWAYS REFER BACK TO (WITCH) DOCTOR...

Health REPORT Best idea whose time has come

On individual suffering that comes with a degenerative disease., Or penniless vegetating old; old people who wish to end their lives. "It's pretty ghoulish when people shoot themselves with guns ETC." knowledgeable in all aspects of "Terminal mercy"

FREEDOM OF CHOICE From human misery!

"provide a humane alternative, Create a pill." DR. SUNDAY

HARD WORK AND DEDICATION

There's a good chance they're going to recognize him this year!

Newsmakers, *A* 1988 **Editorial** Democracy **Prison** Original, **Waiting to Exhale**. *Announcing* a new **"TRAIN YOUR BRAIN"** COURSE OF STRATEGY: **ON GAMING UNPREDICTABiLiTY!** **ARTICLES** **Refresher Course Revisited.** $ **Games** PEOPLE PLAY

SELF-IMPROVEMENT

Guidelines: Read, Listen and Win! `IN GAMBLING, IT'S BETTER TO RECEIVE THEN GIVE! BETTING ON PIG SKINS OR PORK BELLIES, PLAYED BY KINGS & COWBOYS., MANY A RELIGIOUS CONDEMNER OF GAMBLING HAVE LOST TONS OF MONEY IN THA STOCK MARKET., IN THAT 20, YEARS LATER UP-DATE, SPOT ON! J-WALKING IN HEAVY TRAFFIC IS A RISKY GAMBLE., DRIVING WHILE USING A CELL-PHONE OR TEXTING WHILE DRIVING ETC, IS BIG TIME GAMBLING ETC ...

may 1988, RIPPED FROM THE SKY, *obey laws of God.*

On Personal Money Management

"WINNING A CASINO JACK-POT IS LIKE GETTING A FREE CASH MONEY LOAN THAT VOLUNTARILY SOME PEOPLE WILL PAY BACK WITH ENTRUST!

"CASINOS, ARE FUN AND EXCITING PLACES OF VENTURE FOR ANY RESPONSIBLE BILL PAYING ADULT, THAT KNOWS THA TRUE VALUE OF WHAT ONE CAN AFFORD TO WAGER BEFORE MAKING A "FOOL" OF ONESELF., IN THAT EVERYTHING IN LIFE IS TO A DEGREE. WHEREAS THIS IS THA TYPE OF DISCIPLINE ONE MUST ACQUIRE TO WITHHOLD A **POSITIVE** Self Esteem!" *A time for* reflection **New system** **no excuses**.

'JUST THA FACTS'

HAPPY NEW YEAR, 365:
—BARSTOOL SPECTACULAR
Puts You in tha Driver's Seat!

A LITTLE DAB WILL DO YA, IS A HIGHER FORM OF INTELLIGENCE. PROJECTING MIND OVER MATTER, AS OPPOSE TO INTOXICATING MATTER OVER MIND! PRETENTIOUSLY, THIS MAN'S RELIGION IS INTO (CLONING)

WORDS IN THEIR MOUTHS. RE-MONSTRA-TIVELY FALLING PREY TO LETTING YOUR SHOULDER DEVIL TAKE THA WHEEL, CAN RESULT INTO SOME HORRIFYING CIRCUMSTANCES. EXCESSIVE USE OF ALCOHOL WHILE DRIVING IS LIKE - WHO NEEDS A SEAT-BELT WHEN YOU'RE ALREADY EMOTIONALLY STRAPPED TO THA HORSE BLINDER (WOE IS ME) D.U.I. DEATH DEFYING (SELF-CENTERED-SIN-DROME!) LIKEWISE TOSS IN THA DUMB AS MUD, CAREFREE DRIVING (SELF-CENTERED) IMPAIRED INDIVIDUALS FOR A KICKER. CARD HOLDERS CLUB 'SHOWCASE EXPOSURE' ANSWERS TO WHAT'S REALLY HAPPENING BEHIND THESE TRAGIC SCENES.

Get an education that gets you somewhere. An exclusive book excerpt.

MAKING THIS WORLD A BETTER PLACE THEN ONE FOUND IT. BREAKING IT TO THEM GENTLY SIGNED: YOURS TRULY, ANTI-JESUS. 'BOOK'S REGULARITY, ..."AND DEAR GOD, NO NEED TO FORGIVE ANYONE NOW; FOR THEY NOW KNOW WHAT THEY DO! INITIATORLY THROUGH THIS 'BOOK I BELIEVE MY GOD-GIVEN TALENT, WAS MENT TO BE SHARED, AND THAT "THE POSITIVE" WORKS -- THROUGH -- ALL -- MAN -- KIND!!! IN RETROSPECT INSTILLING RESPONSIBILITY ANYONE??? "DEVIL IN THA DETAILS— NOWHERE TO HIDE".

What's News ? PAGE 80

'Shock and awe Bible revision Caveman Extremists Smoke and Mirrors Roll Over Convention— CLEARANCE-SALE — Showstopper.'

((VERSUS)) WITH, OR WITHOUT YOU. THE YOURS TRULY, NEW-AGE, MODERN-DAY, UP-DATED ETERNAL BIBLE! SIGNED: MR. NICE GUY

"Presenting GOD'S INSPIRED WORD."

""WHEN YOUR DOGMA QUITS BARKING""

FREEDOM OF CHOICE' IS FOR YOU TO PREACH 'MY GOSPEL AND KEEP ALL $$$ YOUR PARISHIONERS, OR SUFFER THA CONSECQUNCES OF HEAVY DUTY COMPETITION. SIGNED: YOURS TRULY, ANTI-*Jesus*. "NOBODY EVER WANTED TO BE ME".

COMMISSIONED BY GOD, THUS CREATIVE CONTROL, WITH THA PROMOTION OF A NEW-AGE LIVING BIBLE; PAYING HOMAGE TO ALL INSPIRATIONAL AND INGENIOUS PROPHETS. RESTRUCTURING, REWRITING HISTORIC LIFE STORIES. A WORK OF MONUMENTAL RELIGIOUS AND POLITICAL SIGNIFICANCE; WITH FORMULA TO PROPHECY = DECLARED DEAD AWAKEN TO A NEW LIFE...

Positive news

<u>WEIGHT FOR ME</u>:

YOURS TRULY "1st, TO PROMOTE THIS FORMULAIC COMMONSENSE DIET.")))

LIVING LIFE IN THA FAST FOOD LANE?

`INTRODUCING THA DR. SUNDAE, Diet!"

`YOU GET TO EAT EVERYDAY LIKE IT'S THANKSGIVING., SO DEPENDING ON YOUR OVER-ALL CALORIE INTAKE, ONE MAY ONLY HAVE TO DO UP TO 3 TO 4 HRS, OF HIT THA GROUND RUNNING, <u>DAILY</u> PHYSICAL FITNESS ACTIVITY, TO COMPENSATE!

"PRODUCTS OF OUR ENVIRONMENT."

((NEW AGE PRAYER)) —people—

THEY COME IN ALL KINDS OF COLORS, SHAPES AND SIZES. (SITUATIONALLY SPEAKING) BE NICE TO THEM—

ONE- ~~SIZE~~ `MIND FITS ALL!

ALL CONTRIBUTING TO A **contagious**—philosophy

"I WANT TO LIVE IN A WORLD WHERE <u>VANITY</u> BECOMES THA WORSE SIN ON THA PLANET., BECAUSE THEN ALL PIGGIES, WILL HAVE BECOME NON-EXISTENT."

AUTHOR'S NOTE: IN ALL REALITY THA BEST DIET IS REALLY THA SWISS CHEESE DIET! —YOU JUST EAT THA HOLES...

Kinder? Gentler?

STOP THA WORLD— I WANT TO GET ON! **LEARN ABOUT** FREEDOM OF PROMOTIONAL RELIGIOUS & POLITICAL EXPRESSION, Honoring Divine Inspiration? **Bringing To Life** Criticism ignored by tha media! SIGNED YOURS TRULY, CONGRESSIONAL MEDAL OF HONOR WINNER IN THA WAR OF THA COLD SHOULDER. —— I'M STILL —— —AWAITING YOUR RETURN CALL?

=== OR RESPONSE === NETWORKS = FOX, CNN, NBC, ABC, CBS, NATION-WIDE LETTERS TO THA EDITOR: MORALLY OBLIGATED AMERICA; OR WORLD...

The POSITIVE SPIRIT long reach:

YOURS TRULY, IN BRIEF ON BECOMING CAR-CZAR SALESMAN OF THA YEAR? -OR HOW I BECOME SAVIOR OF THA AUTO INDUSTRY! I'D RE-MAKE, RETROFIT, BRING BACK 'ALL THA MUSCLE CARS ETC, OF THA 50's + 60's, PRICED WITHIN REASON, THEY'D ALL SELL LIKE HOT-CAKES...

JAMAICA MY DAY.

Call me today I specialize in solutions.

Calendar of Events

STORY-LINE 1980, *featuring* CONSECUTIVE YEARS!

THA BATTLE AGAINST TIME.

TV Job Fair program proposal 'It's My Party'. TELEVISION MINISTRY All this & More ! Get ready for truth support. you'll love New On thaTube, Tha DR. Sunday, tape Television shows !!

A different kind of church

Laying Claim to Ministry of Higher Education

discover where you fit in PAGE 83

TAPE. Live from Reno, it's Showtime!

PLAN ON RECORD-BREAKING TELEVISION!

WHAT'S IN STORE? WATCH HIM RISE FROM THA DEAD, MASSIVE AUDIENCES OF PEOPLE THAT WERE BOORED TO DEATH, WITH STATEMENTS LIKE "IF I'M VIRTUALLY HONEST ENOUGH TONIGHT 'I SHOULD BE ABLE TO END FREEDOM OF SPEACH!"

programs promote variety

DON'T UNDERESTIMATE

Get ready for fantastic shows. PROGRAMING :

What's Up Doc? PODIUM SEGMENT. WEEKLY NEWS & REVIEW, ACCORDING TO AUTHOR'S CREDENTIALS. ((COMEDY SEGMENT.)) TRUCK LOADS OF YOURS TRULY WRITTEN SKITS, ACTING WITH GUEST. ((FATHER THYME, COOKING SEGMENT.)) OVER-ALL SPECIALTY COOKING, ALONG WITH OPEN HOUSE CONTEST BY YOURS TRULY, WITH GUEST. ((MUSIC SEGMENT.)) = AN OCCASIONAL BRING DOWN THA HOUSE AND SENATE, ROCK 'N ROOL = BLUES SINGING 'BY YOURS TRULY. TALK SHOW GUEST SEGMENT—MAILBAG RESPONSE SEGMENT.

REVIEW & OUTLOOK **Ready to a-maze you.** no ?→

RENO'S BEST TOURIST ATTRACTION!

iF

BOOK REVIEW

"TESTIMONIALS:

My BOOK SHOULD SELL!

or DEVIL FORBID, "IF ENOUGH PEOPLE CRY WOLF."

written OPINION COMMENTARY

15-CENTURIES of UP in coming FAME,

OUTTA THIS WORLD AND ON WITH THA NEXT!!!

FOR THA LOVE OF ~~MONEY~~ GOD, everything's going to be ALRIGHT.

And They Lived Happily Ever After"...

BETTER LIVING THROUGH DISCOVERY

freedom calls for competition.'

Critics Investigation shows

they're running out of excuses

" The Gospel according to **If you Build This** "

THEY'LL BE A RECTITUDE'L OF

THA NOODLE BY WAY OF

MYSTICAL ENLIGHTENMENT...

When show Business Met Dr. Sunday

Interview factory original

(Transmission in prayer)

OH GOD, CAN YOU HEAR ME NOW???

Question: DO I BELIEVE IN MIRACLES?

His Story ANSWER: WELL, SORT OF!

"I COULD NEVER REMEMBER HIS NAME BUT, THERE ONCE WAS THIS BALD HEADED GUY I KNEW, WITH A SEVERE CASE OF CRIPPLING ARTHRITIS; AND HE ASKED ME TO PRAY FOR HIM. (SO I DID!) AND HE ENDED UP WITH A FULL HEAD OF HAIR."

TESTIMONY TO GOOD LIVING IN

A PERFORMANCE ARTIST!

WHY ME?

Let's start with

ROAD Travels Memorabilia

"YOU KNOW YOU'VE GOT NICE GUY WRITTEN ALL OVER YOUR FACE, WHEN YOUR DRIVING IN A BRISK MOVING FLOW OF RUSH HOUR TRAFFIC AND ROAD SIDE, AN IMPATIENT DOG DARTS INFRONT OF YOUR VEHICLE...

'LABELED BY SOME, TO FUNNY TO BECOME PRESIDENT.'

"HONESTLY SPEAKING"

--- AND I PROMISE I'LL

PUT A JIVE*-TURKEY IN

EVERY HOUSEHOLD ---

NOT BEING THAT
CULTURALLY INFORMED
ABOUT THA AFGAN PEOPLE
AT THAT TIME; THA FIRST
TIME I HAD EVER HEARD THA
WORD 'PASHTUN, I THOUGHT
THEY WERE TALKING ABOUT
SOME KIND OF NEW SHADE
OF WOMENS LIPSTICK! IN
OTHER WORDS - AAA-BOO
 -DABEE-DOO- SHE'S
WEARING 'PASHTUN...

IN FORMULATING A
PRESIDENTIAL EXPLORATORY
COMMITTEE ON A MENIAL
INCOME, I WENT TO THA
 PUB, BOUGHT THA HOUSE A
ROUND, TOLD THEM ABOUT
MY ENDEAVOR, AND THEY
ALL TOLD ME TO GO FOR
IT; SO THEN I ORDERED
THEM A SECOND ROUND,
AND THEY ALL TOLD ME
THAT I WAS GOING TO
BECOME A TWO TERM
PRESIDENT...

PICTURE WAS TAKEN ON
THANKSGIVING '09

* A JIVE TURKEY = IS A LIKEABLE COMEDIC PERSON!

(ONCORE FOLLOW-UP OF SECULAR UP-STAGE!!!)

ANTI-JESUS (VERSUS) JESUS.

" JESUS STATED, LOVE YOUR ENEMIES." " ANTI-JESUS STATES, MAKE
FRIENDS WITH YOUR ENEMIES AND YOUR ENEMIES WILL LOVE YOU."

"BE THIS HERE RESULTING FROM ONE'S LACK OF DIPLOMATIC SKILLS, OR FROM
PLAIN OLD AGGRESSION; - ANYONE WHO HAS EVER DIED IN A WAR - DIED FOR
OUR SINS, ETC.

YOURS TRULY, CHALLENGING ORGANIZED RELIGIONS TO MAKE THA WORLD A BETTER PLACE
WITH PARAMOUNT 24/7 = NEW-AGE LENT, OR FASTING !!!

ONE MUST SACRIFICE HIS OR HERS OWN,

`INSTIGATION OF VERBAL OR PHYSICAL,

INCONSIDERATION TOWARDS OTHERS, TO CONSIDERATION'

- OR JUST BY WAY OF LEAVING WELL ENOUGH ALONE."

AUTHOR'S NOTES: 2011, SENATE HEARING ON ELDERLY ABUSE!
MY TWITTER RESPONSE WAS; "STOP ELDERLY ABUSE, KEEP SOCIAL
SECURITY SOLVENT! = "TAKE THA SCARY OUT OF LIFE! WITH ALL
THIS RUN-AWAY INFLATION TAKING HOLD; WE SURE COULD USE A
FAST-LANE GOVERNMENTAL COST OF LIVING ADJUSTMENT MIRACLE,
TO COUNTER! AMEN...

According to

"Observations, confessions and revelations"

"AS I STATED IN LIFE, I'LL STATE BY WAY OF MY PASSING;
DON'T PRAY TO 'ME --- 'PRAY TO GOD" ...

THERE'S NO BETTER TIME, OR BETTER PLACE

((for **His** legacy set in stone.))

LORD KNOWS

Tell It Like It Is

If I were a rich man...

speaking out On Controversial Issues IN AMERICA

NATION-WIDE

Letters to tha Editor ETC,

QUALITY OF LIFE proposals,

Live from tha cemetery
Set my news free.

Step by Step Book **Check Points** REASON # PAGE 84

Tha big picture In Testimony Whereof

HERE'S LOOKING AT YOU KID, FROM MY GRAVE-STONE EPITAPH.

With ALL MY, OVER-ALL PROPOSED BENEFICIAL CONTRIBUTIONS,
TOWARDS THA BETTERMENT OF MANKIND; OF ALL THA FLESH AND
BLOOD PEOPLE, THAT HAVE EVER SET FOOT ON THIS PLANET!

---"I WOULD HAVE CHOSE TO BE ME!"

THIS BOOK'S PROGRAM DEVELOPMENT WAS ALL DONE WITHOUT THA
USE OF ANY PERFORMANCE ENHANCING (H.G.H.) STEROIDS, OR DRUGS.

now, How do you like me?

miracle on 34th page

ARE WE THERE YET?

Your Audience Needs to Know!

Happenings Around Town

PAGE MY SANITY.

ARE PEOPLE TREATING YOU LIKE AN ALIEN?

"IN THIS MAN'S RELIGION THERE'S GOD IN MAN, BUT THERE'S NO SUCH THING AS A MAN THAT'S GOD!"

*Without **TRUTH** our world could not go on.*

*Church of Open Door **MINISTER***

THiN LiNE PoNTiFF

THA BUNNY ONE THATS GOING TO GET US OUT OF THA JUNGLE HOPPED UP WITH ALL THA GOOD HABiTS, THAT WiLL DO MY BEST NOT TO POOP OUT ON YOU, SO SHARE THE FAiTH AND I HOPE TO BE (TV) N.B.C'iNG YOU SOON.

SIGNED official :

A B C'er of RoBoT SCHOOL.

People in Support.

Tha Beginning: A Friendship That Became A Corporation.

RELIABLE one? GIVE THEM ALL TO JESUS, WHY ME! I DON'T BELONG IN YOUR WORLD •

WARNING: **TO PROTECT LIFE** **CAUTION IS ADVISED** **WARNING:**

TO RUSSiAN, OR MARTiAN AND CELEBRATE STRUCTURED MAN iS DOOMS DAY FUNERAL HOME., BECAUSE THERE'S ONLY ONE God, REELiNG iN THE DiViNE LiGHT LiNE, OUT OF SiGHT POSiTiVE SPIRiT iN THE SKY ...

Fighting tha System Everywhere, Look At Tha Evidence!

WITH A LIST OF FEATURES THIS LONG,

"Looking Back At"

(((Proposed projects)))

If not this, what?
If not now, when?

Dear America, READ This FOR YOURSELF: DID YOU EVER GET THA FEELING YOUR VOTE IS A WASTE OF TIME AND ENERGY, IN THAT YOUR POSITIVE OPINION IS LEFT BEHIND CLOSED DOORS? PAGE 86, MY CONGRESSMAN.

WE'RE NOT GONNA TAKE IT Any more

BEGINS HERE!

"Anatomy of a Revolution".

Liberty

Concepts For Positive Living

AN AMERICAN DOCUMENT

DIFFERENT VIEWS

Experience Insight from ONE of the Most Gifted Visionaries

PREPARING FOR

The REAL world

answers to "Peace On Earth Sale"

ENGINEERED TO a MANHATTAN ISLAND $24. Plus TAX

Smart&Final Testimony!

JUNE 2011, BOOK'S 31st ANNIVERSARY:

"R-E-A-L-I-S-T-I-C
<u>A-R-M-A-G-E-D-D-O-N</u>
A-N-Y-O-N-E"
`GOBALLY SPEAKING, RECOGNIZING THAT
IF YOU WILL,WE'RE AT WAR WITH
'GODZILLA, SATAN, AND OR THE DEVIL,
ANYONE? 'BECAUSE IF YOU WON'T;
WAKE UP AND SMELL THE BARRAGE OF
ON GOING DISASTERS THAT HAVE BEEN
TAKING PLACE! DEMONIC
FLOODS,TORNADOS,EARTHQUAKES, ETC.

YOUR CHOICE!
ONE NATION UNDER GOD.
(OR)
ONE NATION UNDER GODZILLA.

IN CONCLUSION BOOK'S
'REVEALED REVELATION REVOLUTION'
(ALL THIS AND MORE)

EITHER BECOMES GOD'S ENLIGHTEN
TRIUMP OVER EVIL;
(OR)
CAST YOUR VULNERABLE FATE
OFF TO A DEMONIC HAPPENSTANCE...
SIGNED: THE MESSENGER.

Winning Edge